The Oz

Scrapbook

By
David L. Greene
and
Dick Martin

Random House   New York

Library of Congress Cataloging in Publication Data

Greene, David L. , 1944-
The Oz scrapbook.

Bibliography: p.
1. Baum, Lyman Frank, 1856-1919. The wonderful
Wizard of Oz. 2. Baum, Lyman Frank, 1856-1919—
Adaptations. I. Martin, Dick, 1925-   II. Title.
PS3503.A923W634   813′.4   77-3675
ISBN 0-394-41054-8

Manufactured in the United States of America
2 4 6 8 9 7 5 3
First Edition

Design: Robert Aulicino

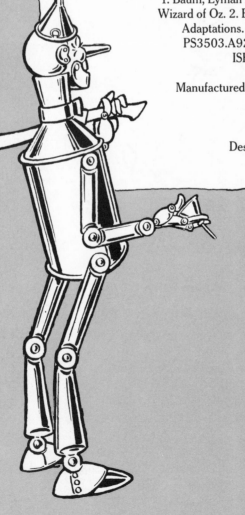
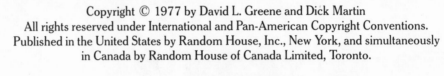

Contents

Preface

The *Wonderful Wizard of Oz* is America's greatest fairy tale, and Oz is its best-loved fairyland. Oz has remained triumphant for over three quarters of a century, in a long series of books; in stage plays and musicals; in movies stretching back to the earliest days of silents through Metro-Goldwyn-Mayer's 1939 classic; in scholarly studies of its author L. Frank Baum and his creation; in toys, games, comic books and practically every other sort of product imaginable. Oz and its inhabitants have become a part of American vocabulary; every public figure from William Randolph Hearst to Everett Dirksen seems to have been likened at one time to the humbug Wizard, while the word "Oz" itself has become synonymous with wondrous, faraway places. Dorothy and her comrades are immortals, existing independently of the book in which they first appeared, and for countless readers, the fairyland through which they journey is a very real place, certainly no less real for being imaginary.

Oz has become an integral part of the American consciousness primarily because it represents the rural America that still dominated the nation at the turn of the century when Dorothy arrived in fairyland. The Land of Oz is the American farm made magical, with a living Scarecrow, a talking hen, a flying dishpan, a copper man made of clockwork, and a witch who melts away like brown sugar. *The Wonderful Wizard of Oz* was published during a time of populists and progressives and Utopian schemes based on an optimistic view of man that, after two world wars, is attractive today precisely because it is so hard to accept. In Oz, good motives, ingenuity and trust in oneself always win, although the way to victory is often rough. Oz is a proving ground in which Dorothy and the other child heroes and heroines develop these quintessentially American ideals.

As a fantasy world, Oz is part of traditions that stretch back to the dawn of storytelling. But Oz is also a very American fairyland, and while it has its monarchies, it has few of the medieval trappings of European fairy tales or of most modern fantasy. As befits a fairyland developed during the progressive era, it is a country where technology is at home, and this too has helped to make it a part of the American consciousness. Instead of including the airplanes and automobiles that he might have but didn't (doubtless because he realized that a fairyland shouldn't be too modern), Baum suggests that magic itself is comprised of technology and scientific investigation. In his final Oz book, *Glinda of Oz,* published in 1920, the most potent magic works a huge machine of gears and wheels. The sense that there is a scientific basis to magic —which Baum never felt it necessary to explain—fits surprisingly well with the rural virtues and scenery amid which the main characters have their adventures. The mechanistic elements in *Glinda of Oz* point toward modern science fiction, in which fantasy becomes scientific extrapolation and the technology of magic is explained. It is perhaps not surprising that when American astronomers recently attempted to monitor communications from intelligent beings elsewhere in the universe, they called it Project Ozma.

By the time L. Frank Baum died in 1919, the Oz series was so popular and the tradition of a new Oz book each year was so important in American homes that his publishers continued the series with other authors. A new Oz book was published each year through 1942; thereafter new books appeared irregularly through 1963. The nineteen Oz books by Baum's immediate successor, Ruth Plumly Thompson, were nearly as popular when they were first published as the original titles.

Beginning with the 1902 *Wizard of Oz* musical comedy on Broadway, Oz has made an amazing variety of appearances on stage and screen—in silent movies, including several produced by Baum himself in 1914, in radio programs, television shows, cartoons, and so on. The 1939 *Wizard of Oz* movie brought stardom to Judy Garland and introduced a new generation to Oz. In the 1970's the all-black musical *The Wiz* became a smash hit on Broadway.

The most surprising aspect of the Oz phenomenon is that, until recently, it was critically disparaged when it wasn't neglected. Many theories have been proposed to explain the rough treatment Oz received at the hands of critics (especially librarians and teachers). Martin Gardner has made the astute observation that there has always been a tendency to deplore a children's series for the nonliterary reason that placing one volume in a library generally obliges the librarian to stock the entire series—and there are forty Oz books. It may also be that Oz suffered from the general rejection of rural values by many intellectuals immediately following World War I. Somewhat later, children's literature developed its own Agrarian Movement, but by then critical opinion had turned against fantasy because it wasn't "true to life." During the past twenty years, critics have reversed themselves completely, and serious articles that recognize Baum as one of America's most important writers for children and the Oz books as major literary achievements have been appearing with increasing frequency. Oz has been analyzed from every point of view from the mythic to the psychoanalytic, the economic, the nostalgic. *The Wizard* is now read in many schools. And although Baum laughed at the academic world as personified by his famous character Professor H. M. Woggle-Bug, T. E., he would have been proud that in 1963 on his birthday, May 15, one of Chicago's new elementary schools was christened the L. Frank Baum School.

The popularity of Oz shows no sign of diminishing. *The Wizard of Oz* has outsold all other American children's books, and it is available today in innumerable editions; the annual television appearances of the 1939 *Wizard* movie have enabled more people to see it than any other motion picture. Editions of *The Wizard* have appeared in every major language; Russia even has its own series of original Oz books by Alexandr Volkov. Enthusiasm among collectors is growing, and first editions of the Oz books, especially the early ones with their elaborate color plates, command high prices; major Baum collections are being formed or acquired by large institutions. (Oz bibliography is very complex, and collectors should consult *Bibliographia Oziana, A Concise Bibliographical Checklist of the Oz Books by L. Frank Baum and His Successors*; it is a definitive account by experts.)

Not least among recent developments has been the success of the International

PORTRAIT OF THE WIZARD OF OZ.

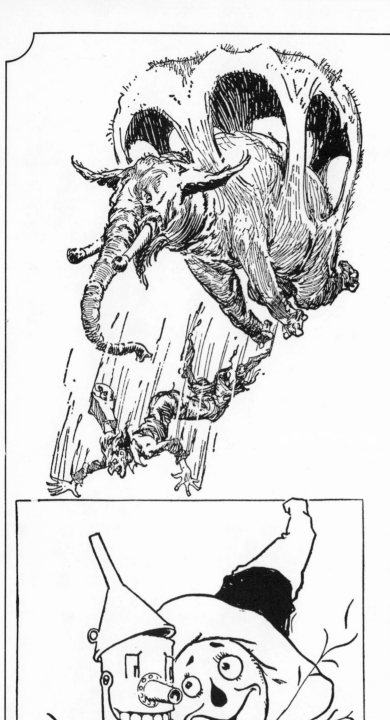

Wizard of Oz Club, a society of Oz enthusiasts, which has been crucial in the growing acceptance of Oz as significant literature and which published the *Bibliographia*. The Oz Club was founded with sixteen charter members in January 1957 by Justin Schiller, a thirteen-year-old Brooklyn boy who is today a leading dealer in rare children's books. The first issue of the club's magazine, *The Baum Bugle*, appeared in four mimeographed pages in June 1957. Justin turned the organization over to others in 1961. Today it has a membership of over 1,600, publishes three periodicals, and sponsors conventions throughout the country. *The Baum Bugle*, which appears three times each year, is a graceful and professional magazine of scholarship and comment on all matters Baumian and Ozian. It is a sign of the organization's ability to smile at itself and its subject—a willingness that goes far to explain the respect in which the magazine is held outside the club—that the Bugle has retained the irrelevant, alliterative title chosen for the first tentative issue sent to sixteen members two decades ago. (Memberships, including *The Baum Bugle*, are $5 a year from the International Wizard of Oz Club, P.O. Box 95, Kinderhook, Ill. 62345.)

The Oz Scrapbook is an attempt to provide an overview of the entire amorphous phenomenon of Oz. In showing its manifestations, from important fantasies to frivolous spin-offs, we have had to exercise great and somewhat arbitrary selectivity. We hope that the text and photographs, limited as they are, will remind readers of the time when Dorothy and her comrades helped them see the magic that was not only beyond the Deadly Desert but also in everyday things. Surely this is something we all need to be reminded of.

DAVID L. GREENE
DICK MARTIN

The Man Who Discovered Oz

Chapter
1

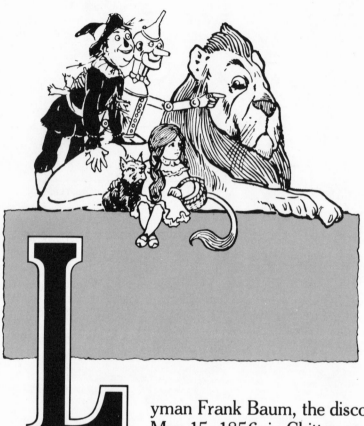

Lyman Frank Baum, the discoverer of Oz, was born on May 15, 1856, in Chittenango, New York. His father, Benjamin Ward Baum, was a man of humble origin who had made a fortune in the Pennsylvania oil fields. Four years after Frank's birth the family moved to the outskirts of Syracuse, where they lived in considerable luxury at a country estate Mrs. Baum christened "Rose Lawn." Frank spent most of his childhood there. Rose Lawn is mentioned by name in his 1901 fantasy, *Dot and Tot of Merryland,* and the Emerald City may owe some of its opulence to the estate. In his adult life, Baum used Rose Lawn as a standard of living against which he judged his failures and accomplishments.

Young Frank was indulged by his family, partially because he had a weak heart and also because his parents wanted to spare their children the rigors of their own childhoods. In one major way, however, Frank was not indulged: Benjamin Baum, who shared with other well-to-do fathers of the time the view that boys should go to military school, sent his son to the Peekskill Military Academy in 1868. After the indulgences of Rose Lawn, Frank was miserable during his two years at Peekskill. Finally, the rigors of military life brought on a seizure usually described as a heart attack. Baum was surely thinking of his own experiences at Peekskill when

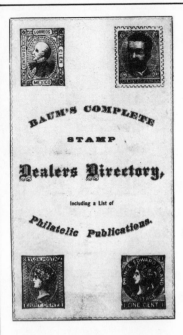

Baum as a twelve-year-old cadet
at military academy.

he ridiculed military men and academics in the Oz books. One of the contradictions of his life is that in later years he sent three of his sons to the Michigan Military Academy.

The multiplicity of Baum's interests was evident in his boyhood. Benjamin Baum had the resources to cater to his son's wishes, so the boy was able to go further with his hobbies than most children. When he was fifteen his father bought him a printing press, and for three years Frank and a younger brother issued a newspaper called *The Rose Lawn Home Journal*. When he was about seventeen Frank and a friend began a paper called *The Empire*, which featured, among various topics, news about postage stamps. In 1873 he published a directory of stamp dealers.

The strongest of his early interests was drama. With his father's financial support he became an actor when he was in his early twenties, using at various times the names "Louis F. Baum" and "George Brooks." Family tradition, as reported in Russell P. MacFall's biography of Baum, *To Please a Child*, is that he was first hired by a Shakespearean troupe so that the players could borrow permanently the fine stock of costumes with which his father had provided him.

Baum as Hugh Holcomb in his own melodrama, *The Maid of Arran* (1886). Above, a souvenir cover. (Courtesy American Literature Collection, Beinecke Rare Book and Manuscript Library, Yale University)

It is easy, in this modern psychoanalytic era, to blame a man's life on his childhood. Yet there is evidence that much of Baum's life was colored by his early years at Rose Lawn, where he had found life easy. In his early adulthood he tried an amazing variety of professions, abandoning each when it turned out not to be so easy as he had expected, or when it became evident that he had not paid enough attention to its financial ramifications. During his early and middle twenties he was an actor, playwright, manager of theaters owned by his father, newspaper reporter in Pennsylvania and New York City, and salesman. He left each profession, though he was later to go back to most of them, with the knowledge that his father's money would support him.

In 1882 Baum seemed to find his niche. He wrote an Irish melodrama, *The Maid of Arran,* and formed a theatrical company which performed the play for two years. As Louis F. Baum, he played the lead and wrote not only the play itself but also the words and music of the songs.

The Maid of Arran is based on William Black's now-forgotten novel, *A Princess of Thule.* In keeping with the theatrical expectations of the period, Baum moved the action from Scotland to Ireland, and for a stage dominated by *East Lynn* and the melodramas of Dion Boucicault, created a sentimental tear-jerker out of a relatively restrained story. To the modern reader The *Maid of Arran* is so absurd that it is delightful, and it helps us understand, if not excuse, the occasional sentimentality of the Oz books.

The Maid of Arran was very much a family affair. One of Baum's aunts had a major part, his uncle was the manager, and the play was undoubtedly financed by Benjamin Baum. The production was favorably received, with a June 1882 engagement in New York City, a Chicago engagement that October, and a tour that took the com-

pany as far west as Nebraska and as far north as Ontario. Almost every review praised the production, especially Baum's acting ability. But financially the play was a failure.

On November 9, 1882, Baum married Maud Gage of Fayetteville, New York, a daughter of the redoubtable Matilda Joslyn Gage, who was, with Elizabeth Cady Stanton and Susan B. Anthony, a leading suffragist. Maud was able to provide some stability throughout their married life, despite her husband's lifelong propensity for getting into financial difficulties. It was a very happy marriage.

In the next six years two sons were born, Frank Joslyn and Robert Stanton. Baum was delighted by fatherhood. He had an inborn ability to please children, and he exercised his fertile imagination in countless stories. During most of this period he was working in the family oil business, primarily in the manufacture of Baum's Castorine, an axle grease. His financial bad luck continued: a combination of circumstances reduced Benjamin Ward Baum's wealth considerably before his death in 1887, and in 1888 it was discovered that a clerk had embezzled most of the capital of the Castorine company. Frank made the romantic decision to try to make a living in Aberdeen, in what was shortly to become South Dakota. In the meantime, he had published his first book, a seventy-page disquisition on raising chickens entitled *The Book of the Hamburgs* (1886).

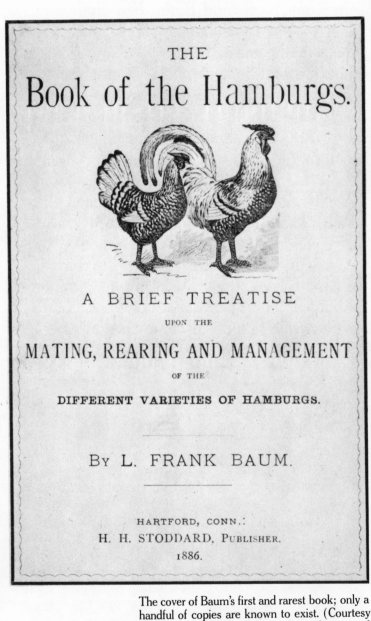

THE
Book of the Hamburgs.

A BRIEF TREATISE

UPON THE

MATING, REARING AND MANAGEMENT

OF THE

DIFFERENT VARIETIES OF HAMBURGS.

By L. FRANK BAUM.

HARTFORD, CONN.:
H. H. STODDARD, PUBLISHER.
1886.

The cover of Baum's first and rarest book; only a handful of copies are known to exist. (Courtesy The New York Public Library, Astor, Lenox and Tilden Foundations)

L. Frank Baum, as he was now calling himself, had been the principal salesman of the Castorine company, so when the family moved to Aberdeen in September 1888, he decided to try his luck behind the counter of a variety store he named Baum's Bazaar. At first there seemed to be every opportunity for the business to grow, but times got hard, and Baum had charitably allowed too much credit. The bank foreclosed at the end of 1889.

He next became publisher of a weekly newspaper, *The Aberdeen Saturday Pioneer*, of which he assumed control in January 1890. It is hard to imagine how he thought he could make a go of it, for Aberdeen already had two daily and seven weekly newspapers, but Baum edited the *Pioneer* with enthusiasm, writing witty verse and editorials, and a column called "Our Landlady." The central figure in the column is Mrs. Bilkins, the fictitious proprietor of an Aberdeen boarding house. "Our Landlady" is filled with humorous comments on Aber-

deen people and on the word in general; it shows that Baum had developed considerably as a writer since his *Arran* days. In one column Mrs. Bilkins describes the elaborate uniforms of the Aberdeen girls' marching troupe—the probable source for Glinda's elaborately garbed female soldiers in the Oz books. In another week's installment a farmer tells the landlady that he has put

The rare first edition of the book that started it all. (Courtesy Peter E. Hanff)

green spectacles on his horses so they will think that they're eating grass rather than wood shavings; ten years later the Wizard used green glasses to make people believe everything in the Emerald City was green, and the drought that forced the farmer to deceive his livestock is described movingly in the opening chapter of *The Wonderful Wizard of Oz.*

Baum lost the *Pioneer* at the end of March 1891; years later he recalled that "the sheriff wanted the paper more than I did." In Aberdeen he had made many friends but had not found a livelihood. He was nearly thirty-five years old and the father of two more sons, Harry Neal and Kenneth Gage.

In the spring of 1891 the Baum family moved to Chicago, where Baum was successively a reporter, a buyer for a department store, and a traveling salesman for a crockery firm. Maud's mother, now widowed, was living with the Baums, and a letter from her to another daughter in February 1897 reveals the closeness between Frank and Maud—and something of the strong-minded lady's view of her son-in-law: "L. F. comes in Friday. He failed to receive M's letter for a day or two and telegraphed her—seems he wouldn't travel if he didn't hear, &c &c—a perfect baby." But another letter that spring shows that the older lady was proud that "L. F." was having stories published in a national magazine and had manuscripts for two children's books under consideration by major publishers. Indeed, Baum family tradition is that Mrs. Gage first encouraged him to write down the stories he had for years been telling his sons.

Baum completed the manuscripts for his first two children's books in 1896 and tentatively entitled them *Adventures in Phuniland* and *Tales from Mother Goose.* In 1897, Way & Williams, an important

MOTHER GOOSE IN PROSE.

A Christmas Book for Children. . . .
By L. FRANK BAUM.

• • •

THIS is an entirely new departure in children's literature, Mr. Baum having taken the well-known rhymes of Mother Goose and built around them a series of most charming stories to delight the youngsters. Each of the famous heroes of the nursery is the centre of a tale of adventure of wonderful interest. There are twelve full-page quaint and original drawings by MAXFIELD PARRISH, who has also designed the cover, in six colors.

• • •

FIRST EDITION NEARLY EXHAUSTED.
ORDER NOW.

WAY & WILLIAMS, Publishers, Caxton Building, Chicago.

Sample Illustration from "Mother Goose in Prose."

An advertisement for Baum's first children's book which was also the first book illustrated by Maxfield Parrish. (*Publishers Weekly*, Christmas Bookshelf Number, 1897)

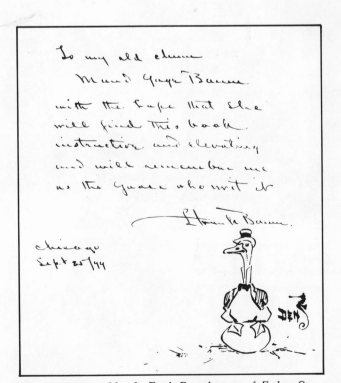

The inscription in Mrs. L. Frank Baum's copy of *Father Goose* from the "Goose who writ it," with a drawing by W. W. Denslow.

8

Mother Goose in Prose was reprinted a number of times, including a twelve-part series of pamphlets for Pettijohn's Breakfast Food in 1901.

The dust jacket for *Father Goose: His Book*, the first Baum-Denslow collaboration and an 1899 best seller. (Courtesy Chicago Historical Society) Above, the front cover design.

Chicago publisher, issued the Mother Goose book as *Mother Goose in Prose,* Not only was *Mother Goose* Baum's first published children's book, it was the first book illustrated by Maxfield Parrish, who within the next decade became America's most popular artist. It was a magnificently produced, large-quarto volume, more important, perhaps, for its illustrations than for its text. Many of Baum's elaborations of traditional nursery rhymes have a regrettable tendency toward sentimentality. In several, however, he anticipates *The Wonderful Wizard of Oz* by sophisticated exposures of humbuggery. Baum's "Phuniland" tales, which finally appeared in 1900 as *A New Wonderland,* are on the whole better than his Mother Goose stories.

Baum, who was essentially a family man, did not enjoy his work as a traveling salesman, even though it provided what he and his family had so often been without: a steady income. Doubtless encouraged by the acceptance of *Mother Goose in Prose.* he persuaded C. L. Williams of Way & Williams to finance *The Show Window,* a magazine for window dressers. *The Show Window* began publication in November 1897 with Baum as editor and was an immediate success. It allowed him to remain at home and pursue his career as an author, and even gave him time to set in type, print and bind in his basement workshop ninety-nine copies of a small collection of his own verse entitled *By the Candelabra's Glare.*

Baum had spent many years feeling his way uncertainly. Now, in his early forties, he had a certain sense of his own future; he would earn his living as a writer. For several years he had known William Wallace Denslow, a newspaper cartoonist and poster designer with a considerable reputation who, since he signed most of his drawings with a stylized sea horse (or *Hippocampus*), was

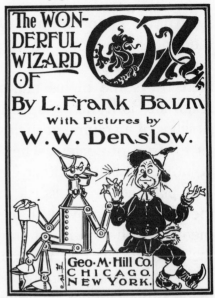
The title page of the first edition.

L. Frank Baum around 1901. The legs at the right probably belong to one of his sons.

W. W. Denslow at work.

known as Hippocampus Den throughout the Bohemian world he frequented. Sometime in 1898 or early 1899, Baum showed Denslow some of his humorous verse for children. Both men were struck by the possibilities of a volume of such verse illustrated as a series of posters. They put together a volume, entitled it *Father Goose: His Book* and planned to publish it themselves. But the financing proved to be beyond their means, so they reached an agreement with the George M. Hill Company, a Chicago book jobber and reprint house which aspired to become a major publishing firm. *Father Goose* appeared in September 1899 and created a sensation in the Chicago publishing world. By the end of 1901, it had sold nearly 60,000 copies.

Although *Father Goose* is a charming volume, it has been forgotten. Baum and Denslow would be forgotten, too, were it not for their next book, *The Wonderful Wizard of Oz.*

The genesis of *The Wizard* is uncertain, although parts of it came from stories Baum had made up for his sons, and surprisingly, the likable Scarecrow originated in his recurring childhood nightmare of being chased by a scarecrow. Early publicity stated that Baum took the word "Oz" from a filing cabinet drawer labeled "O-Z." Denslow later implied that he had helped develop the ideas in the book, and there is evidence that author and illustrator together worked on certain elements of the story that each felt he had the right to after their informal partnership dissolved. But whatever characters or incidents originated with Denslow, *The Wonderful Wizard of Oz* is a great book because of L. Frank Baum. For although Denslow later wrote about Oz characters, he produced nothing of literary value.

The earliest title for the book was apparently *The City of Oz;* it was then called

Did you ever see a rabbit climb a tree? Did you ever see a lobster ride a flea? Did you ever? No, you never! For they simply couldn't do it, don't you see!

A page from *Father Goose.*

The City of the Great Oz, The Emerald City, From Kansas to Fairyland, The Fairyland of Oz and *The Land of Oz*, before it was published by Hill in September 1900 as *The Wonderful Wizard of Oz*. (Despite persistent tradition, *The Wizard* was not a vanity publication, although Baum and Denslow did retain ownership of the printing plates.)

The Wonderful Wizard of Oz is a deceptively simple story. A little girl named Dorothy and her dog, Toto, are carried by a cyclone to the country of the Munchkins (who prefer blue) and she spends the rest of the book trying to get home. On her way to the Emerald City to ask the Wizard, who rules there, for help, she meets a Scarecrow who wants a brain, a Tin Woodman who wants a heart, and a Cowardly Lion who wants courage. After several adventures on the road they reach the city, but the Wizard refuses to grant their wishes until they have destroyed the

When Bobbs-Merrill reprinted *The Wonderful Wizard of Oz* in 1903, the title was changed to *The New Wizard of Oz.* "New" was dropped from the cover and spine almost at once.

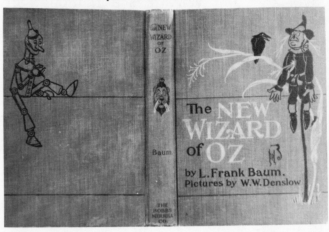

A 1900 poster by Denslow with a goose looking surprised that the Oz characters are getting ahead of him.

Wicked Witch of the West. The comrades then journey to the Country of the Winkies (who prefer yellow), where the witch lives. She tries unsuccessfully to destroy them until Dorothy ultimately (and accidentally) melts her with a bucket of water. When they return to the Emerald City, they discover that the Wizard is a humbug, an American circus balloonist whose balloon had carried him to Oz many years before. Nevertheless, he is able to provide Dorothy's friends with symbols of what they want. He and Dorothy plan to return to the United States in his balloon, but Dorothy is accidentally left behind. Undaunted, she and her companions journey south to ask help of the Good Witch Glinda, ruler of the Quadlings (who prefer red). Glinda does indeed show her how to get home. The Scarecrow becomes ruler of the Emerald City, and the Tin Woodman, emperor of the Winkies. The Cowardly Lion returns to the forest to rule.

The plot of *The Wonderful Wizard of Oz*, like most of Baum's plots, is seriously flawed: the journey to Glinda is anticlimactic. What, then, gives *The Wizard* greatness? Most fairy tales are universal because they occur in distant times and places. Baum achieved universality by combining the folk tale with elements familiar to every child—cornfields, things made of tin, circus balloons. Dorothy is an especially fine creation: a simple child who in the midst of wonders goes matter-of-factly about her business. In his preface Baum describes the book as a "modernized fairy tale, in which the wonderment and joy are retained and the heart-aches and nightmares are left out." Fortunately he did not succeed in leaving out nightmares and heartaches, for without wicked witches and other terrors to be overcome, *The*

The cover of *The Wizard* that was used by Bobbs-Merrill from about 1920 until 1939.

Denslow's Tin Woodman and Scarecrow.

Wonderful Wizard of Oz would be far less than it is.

The Scarecrow and the Tin Woodman are among the greatest grotesques in American literature. They are made human by their very human desires, and Baum supplies many details to render them even more "real." A prime example is the Tin Woodman's tale of how he became tin. He was a man of meat who fell in love with a beautiful girl. The old woman she lived with didn't want to lose the girl's services as cook and housemaid, so she bribed the Wicked Witch of the East to enchant the Woodman's ax. The ax cut off parts of his body, which were replaced by a tinsmith until eventually he was entirely tin. The Scarecrow tells the story of his creation, noting particularly that the farmer who made him painted his left eye larger than his right; three of the Oz illustrators—W. W. Denslow, John R. Neill and Dick Martin—faithfully drew one eye larger than the other, though they were frequently uncertain about which eye. Other small touches, like the Tin Woodman's tendency to rust and the Scarecrow's difficulty in picking berries with his padded fingers, help the reader to accept the two characters.

Oz itself in the first Oz book is different from the fairyland of the later books, in part because Baum did not originally consider the country to be a single entity. The word "Oz," in fact, was the name of the Wizard, not of the country, until Baum made some hasty alterations just before the book went to press. Oz is more dangerous in *The Wizard*. There are dangers aplenty in the later books, but never again are so many living things destroyed or threatened with destruction.

Reviewers recognized at once that *The Wonderful Wizard of Oz* was a major contribution to children's literature. Baum's scrap-

book contains two hundred and two reviews, of which only two are unfavorable. A review in *The Bookseller* for September 1, 1900, was one of many that compared The Wizard favorably with *Alice in Wonderland*. Denslow's illustrations were almost universally admired.

The Wizard sold well, but not so well as *Father Goose* had, probably because Baum hurt himself by publishing too much in the same year. In 1900 he published four other children's books: two alphabet books for the very young; a collection of verses from *Father Goose* set to music by Alberta N. Hall; and *A New Wonderland*.

The next three years were almost as busy. Baum was consciously experimenting with the fairy tale, both to see what could be done with it and to discover what his audience preferred. In 1901 the prestigious Bowen-Merrill Company of Indianapolis published his science-fiction novel for teen-aged boys, *The Master Key: An Electrical Fairy Tale*. During the same year Hill published the final Baum-Denslow book, a slow-moving, nearly plotless fantasy entitled *Dot and Tot of Merryland*, and Baum's *American Fairy Tales*, a series of realistic, cynical stories, some set in contemporary America.

Early in 1902 Hill was forced into bankruptcy, and the Bowen-Merrill Company became Baum's publisher. In 1902 it brought out Baum's *Life and Adventures of Santa Claus*; the next year, under its new name of Bobbs-Merrill, it published his *Enchanted Island of Yew*; a rewritten version of *A New Wonderland* called *The Magical Monarch of Mo*; and *The Wonderful Wizard of Oz* under the title *The New Wizard of Oz*. Copyright Office correspondence examined by Michael Hearn suggests that Bobbs-Merrill changed the title to obtain a copyright on the book as a new edition,

since there was some question about the validity of the 1900 copyright. Denslow's new cover, end paper and title-page designs were the last gasp of the Baum-Denslow partnership. Fights over the 1902 *Wizard of Oz* stage play (see page 118) had ended any pretense of cooperation between the erstwhile friends. Each man now began working independently on ideas for using the Oz characters in future writings, and each felt considerable bitterness toward the other.

Denslow's Scarecrow and Tin-Man on Skates.

Written and Illustrated by W.W. Denslow Illustrator of "The WIZARD OF OZ" and "The PEARL and the PUMPKIN"

COPYRIGHT 1904 BY W.W. DENSLOW
ALL RIGHTS RESERVED.

"My straw stuffing is getting mouldy," said the Scarecrow, as he was being brushed by Buttons, the palace page.

"I'm getting a bit rusty myself," said the Tinman, as he moved his joints with difficulty.

"Say, boys," shouted the Tinman, "let us go skating. The weather is cold and there is plenty of ice."

"I can't skate on this spring," said Jack-in-the-Box; "I haven't any feet."

"That can be fixed all right," said the Scarecrow. "We will ask the blacksmith to give you another spring and make you a

pair of feet. Then you will be a double-footer, and be able to walk or spring just as you choose. We need a good lively man around the palace."

No sooner said than done. The wonderful blacksmith who had once fixed up the Tinman now took Jack in hand, and made for him another spring and a pair (____, ____) he was twice as good as new.

In the crisp, cold morning air the three friends started off to the river, and on arriving at the bank put on their skates. It was

lucky for them all that they could not seriously hurt themselves, for none of the three had ever been on skates before.

The Scarecrow was the first to get them fastened upon his boots, and in a moment was off upon the smooth, glassy ice, but much to his surprise he had great trouble in keeping his balance. His left foot went one way and his right another, until finally his funny capers ended in a long slide on the back of his neck, at which his two companions shouted with mirth. He was soon joined on the ice by the Tinman and Jack, who was very proud of his new feet, and then began the funniest antics ever seen outside of a circus ring.

"He's funnier than a dozen clowns," said a member of the Fresh Air Club, while all the skaters on the distance away a dark sheet of water directly in their path. To stop was impossible, so the three sure of a ducking.

Jack-in-the-Box rose to the situation gloriously by springing lightly into the air with a might that landed him safely on the sound ice beyond the open water. But the unlucky Scarecrow and did not fare so well, and they were soon floundering about on the surface of the icy waves.

A page from Denslow's unsuccessful Sunday comic which ran for a few months in 1904 and 1905.

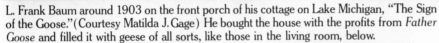

L. Frank Baum around 1903 on the front porch of his cottage on Lake Michigan, "The Sign of the Goose." (Courtesy Matilda J. Gage) He bought the house with the profits from *Father Goose* and filled it with geese of all sorts, like those in the living room, below.

Denslow's earliest independent use of the Oz characters was in a small booklet made up of the Hill color plates for *The Wizard. Pictures from The Wonderful Wizard of Oz* "by W. W. Denslow" was issued around 1903 by George W. Ogilvie & Company of Chicago, with a poor story written by Thomas H. Russell to fit the pictures. In 1904 Denslow began his *Scarecrow and the Tin-Man* comic page, which ran from December 1904 to March 1905 and was apparently carried by very few papers. He also published *Denslow's Scarecrow and the Tin-Man* as one of his series of picture books for the New York publisher G. W. Dilling-

ham. Denslow's text for both the comic page and the picture book is inconsequential.

The variety of books written by Baum from 1900 through 1903 suggests that he was not at first aware of the importance of *The Wizard.* He was encouraged to write more about Oz by the success of the *Wizard* play and by his continuing financial troubles. In 1902 he had resigned his editorship of *The Show Window* in the expectation that he could make his living as a children's author and a dramatist, and during the same year he bought a cottage at Macatawa on Lake Michigan, where his family had spent summers since 1899. These added ex-

penses and continued financial bad luck offset his income from books and from the play of *The Wizard* to such an extent that in 1903 the referee in the Hill bankruptcy agreed that Baum was insolvent. Obviously Baum hoped that another Oz book would correct that condition.

The second Oz book, *The Marvelous Land of Oz*, was published in July 1904 by the Reilly & Britton Company, a new Chicago publishing house. Baum was displeased with the manner in which Bobbs-Merrill had publicized his books, and Reilly & Britton promised to promote them aggressively.

The Marvelous Land of Oz was originally announced with the infelicitous title

The Further Adventures of the Scarecrow and the Tin Woodman, and it is dedicated to Fred Stone and David Montgomery, who played those characters on the stage. Neither Dorothy nor the Cowardly Lion has a role in the book. The central character is Tip, a young boy from the Gillikin Country of Oz reared by a suspected witch named Mombi. One morning Tip makes a wooden figure with a pumpkin for a head and sets it in the road to frighten the old woman. Mombi brings the figure to life with a magical powder she has just acquired and then decides to transform Tip into a marble statue to prevent him from annoying her further. Tip escapes and goes to the Emerald City, taking with him the wooden figure (whom he has named Jack Pumpkinhead) and the Powder of Life. On the way there, he brings a sawhorse to life, and a little later, meets General Jinjur, who has raised an army of

The cover on the first edition of the second Oz book. (Courtesy Peter E. Hanff)

girls to conquer the Emerald City. Various other complications occur; new characters are introduced; and finally, with Glinda in command, Jinjur is defeated by Tip, the Scarecrow, the Tin Woodman and others. What happens next set the direction for the rest of the Oz series: Tip learns that he is really Princess Ozma, the long-lost ruler of Oz, whom the Wizard had given as a baby to Mombi and whom she transformed into a boy. With considerable misgivings, Tip agrees to be restored to his throne and his original form.

The Marvelous Land of Oz was recognized by the early reviewers as a fine book. Many said that it was as good as The Wizard itself. General Jinjur's Army of Revolt is, of course, a satire on the feminist movement, something with which Baum was well acquainted thanks to his mother-in-law. But the book is not anti-feminist. The role changes that Jinjur brings about during her brief rule of the Emerald City are ridiculous, but it is a woman, Glinda, who restores order by bringing another woman, Ozma, to the throne of Oz. Baum recognized women's supreme role in folk tales as wise counselors, great rulers and wicked stepmothers. He was, in fact, laying the groundwork for a fairyland in which women —Ozma, Glinda and various child heroines from America—are supreme, and men support their supremacy. The major flaw in The Marvelous Land of Oz comes from Baum's plans to turn it into a stage play. Unlike the reviewer in the Cleveland Leader for November 6, 1904, most modern readers aren't bothered by the fact that "General Jinjur and her soldiers are only shapely chorus girls. We can see their tights and their ogling glances even in the pages of the book." But it comes as a jolt that Tip is changed into a girl at the end of the book. Dramas of the period were strongly in-

Around 1906 the cover title of the book was shortened, although the title page carried the full title until 1912.

A poster designed by John R. Neill.

fluenced by the English pantomime tradition, in which the leading boy is played by a woman, who appears in female clothing at the end. In preparing for the stage version of *The Land*, Baum hurt the book.

Oz itself is somewhat different from the fairyland of *The Wizard*. The threat of destruction is no longer ever-present, and when it occurs it is usually funny, like Jinjur's decision to turn the Woggle-Bug into "Hungarian goulash, stewed and highly spiced." The only witch is Mombi, and she is hardly of the same caliber as the Wicked Witch of the West. Baum now informs his readers that the northern country of Oz is that of the Gillikins, who prefer purple.

Especially noteworthy among the many virtues of the book are the grotesques. In his stupidity, Jack Pumpkinhead is appealing, and even the Sawhorse is given personality. Mr. H. M. Woggle-Bug, T. E., who joins Tip and his group, is one of Baum's comic masterpieces, the personification of pedantry—"H. M." stands for "Highly Magnified," and "T. E." for "Thoroughly Educated." Mr. Woggle-Bug (he becomes a professor in later books) achieved his education on the hearth of a schoolhouse, and his gigantic size by escaping after the schoolmaster had projected him magnified on a screen for the edification of the pupils. The flying Gump is another superb example of Baum's ability to make the everyday magical; it is composed of two sofas, clothesline, palm branches, rope, and the stuffed head of a gump (in Oz, a gump is an elk-like creature; in Baum's America, as Martin Gardner has pointed out, it was slang for a "stupid fellow").

The Marvelous Land of Oz was only part of a large number of Oz projects developed by Baum and his publishers. The month after the book appeared, Baum sent the Scarecrow, the Tin Woodman, the

This advertisement from *Publishers' Weekly* for September 3, 1904, shows the wide range of promotion for *The Marvelous Land of Oz*.

QUEER VISITORS FROM THE MARVELOUS LAND OF OZ
Introducing the Scarecrow the Tin Woodman and their Comrades
The Fairy Tale by L. Frank Baum
The Pictures by Walt McDougall
Copyright 1904 by L. Frank Baum.

THE SUNDAY RECORD-HERALD COMIC (FOURTH) SECTION
Chicago, Ill., Sunday, January 8, 1905

1 He stood in a corner and kept quiet.

2 The fire bells were ringing and the whistles were blowing.

3 The tin woodman decides to go and help.

4 "Save my darling!"

5 Up through the flames he went

7 The flames drove him back.

6 Carefully holding the flour can.

How the Tin Woodman became a fire hero.

NIGHT was a rather dreary time for our friends, the visitors from the marvelous Land of Oz. For, with the single exception of the Wogglebug, not one of the queer people ever slept. One was straw, and one was tin; one had a carved pumpkin head, and their Sawhorse was made of wood. To such creatures sleep was, of course, an impossibility; but to avoid annoying other folks who DID sleep, they made a practice of standing in the corners of a room with their faces to the wall during all the night, so they might not be tempted to talk or make a noise.

This standing still for so long a time was somewhat tedious, as any child who has tried it will be glad to acknowledge; so that one night, when the bells began clanging, and the whistles tooting they all turned around from their corners with a sigh of relief.

"Some one else is making a racket now," said the Scarecrow. "I wonder what all those bells and whistles mean?"

But before any could answer they heard cries of "Fire! Fire!" coming from the street.

"How dreadful!" exclaimed the Pumpkinhead. "But I dare not go near the fire, because my body is made of wood." And he turned his face resolutely to the wall again.

"Those are exactly my sentiments!" declared the Sawhorse, and poked his nose as far into his corner as it would go.

"For my part," remarked the Scarecrow, "fire has ever been my great abhorrence. Any chance spark might set my straw to burning; and then there would soon be an end of me."

"My case is different," said the Tin Woodman. "I am composed of three-ply metal plate of the best quality, and fire does not worry me in the least. So, if you will excuse me, I'll go and see if I can be of any service."

He walked into the street, and seeing people running in a certain direction, he followed them to a tall apartment building, from the windows of which smoke was pouring in great clouds.

The firemen had already arrived and were shooting streams of water through some of the windows, while across the street were groups of half-dressed people shivering in the cold, who had been driven from their beds by the burning of the house.

As the Tin Woodman joined the crowd of spectators, a very short but very fat woman, with variegated yellow hair and pink cheeks, rushed forward and cried out:

"Oh, my darling; my darling! He will be burned alive!"

"Where is he?" asked a big fireman, excitedly.

"There! There in that corner room!" screamed the woman, pointing to the second story.

At once the fireman placed a ladder against the building, and the big fellow bravely ran up the rounds to the window that the woman had indicated. But a burst of flame and smoke quickly drove him back again, and the woman began dancing hysterically up and down and crying: "My darling will be burned alive!"

"I'm afraid he will," said the fireman, sadly, "for no person can enter that room through the window without being killed."

"I can!" exclaimed the Tin Woodman. "Fear not, my good woman, for I will save your darling!"

A cheer broke from the crowd at hearing this courageous speech. But the Tin Woodman reflected that if a child was in the room he could not carry it out through the flames; so he looked around and discovered a big flour can, which a man had carefully carried downstairs after throwing his clocks and mirrors from the third-story window. So the Tin Woodman grabbed the big round flour can, which was also made of tin, and climbed up the ladder to the window. In through the smoke and raging flames he made his way, and in a few minutes the anxious crowd watching him from below saw him reappear, carefully holding a flour can in his arms.

"Your darling is saved!" shouted the Tin Woodman to the woman; and then a tremendous cheer greeted him as he came down the ladder and reached the ground. For no one but a tin man could ever have passed through the flames in safety, and even he was glowing red in several places where the fire had caught him. The big fireman, who admired bravery, grasped his tin hand with emotion—and dropped it with a howl.

As soon as he was on the ground the Tin Woodman threw off the cover of the flour can, and out jumped a little poodle dog, which the woman caught in her arms.

"Oh, thank you for saving my darling!" she cried, joyfully.

"Your darling!" growled the big fireman, disgusted and angry. "Were you raising all that row over a measly dog?"

"He isn't measly," she simpered; "he's a dear, and a love, and a darling!"

The fireman turned to the Tin Woodman.

"I don't blame you for being hot," he said, indignantly.

"It isn't my honor that's tarnished, anyhow," replied the hero, with a slight sigh; "and if I'm obliged to get myself replated in the morning I shall not complain. For, after all, to the dog and the woman the life I saved is very precious, and I am glad I had the chance to make somebody happy."

But at this kind speech the firemen only frowned.

"You'll feel different when you've cooled off," he said.

L. FRANK BAUM.

8 The redhot handshake.

9 Out jumped a poodle dog

A page from Baum's Sunday comic. The Visitors get into an amazing variety of situations in America. For the first part of the tour, the Woggle-Bug bails them out, to the pleasure of the newspapers that participated in the "What Did the Woggle-Bug Say?" contest.

By the end of 1904 Woggle-Bug fever had reached such proportions that even unrelated products like Hamm's Beer joined in the fun, probably to Baum's surprise.

Woggle-Bug, Jack Pumpkinhead and the Sawhorse to the United States by Gump in a weekly newspaper comic page called *Queer Visitors from the Marvelous Land of Oz,* which ran from August 1904 through February 1905, almost concurrently with Denslow's—a fact that must have increased the bitterness between the two men. *Queer Visitors* was illustrated by Walt McDougall, a well-known political cartoonist for the Philadelphia *North American.* Although Baum's comic page is better written than Denslow's, none of the Visitors' adventures is especially memorable. (The episodes from the page included in Reilly & Lee's 1960 picture book *The Visitors from Oz* were drastically rewritten.)

Nevertheless, *Queer Visitors from the Marvelous Land of Oz* was popular, largely because of a contest connected with the page. Each episode during 1904 featured a problem solved by the Woggle-Bug and ended with the question "What Did the Woggle-Bug Say?" There were prizes for the correct answer. The newspapers that carried the page distributed Woggle-Bug buttons, and the question became a national catch phrase. In fact, when the St. Paul *Dispatch* was publishing the series, the rival *Pioneer Press* ran an advertisement showing the insect quaffing Hamm's Beer; doubtless he was moonlighting without the permission of Baum, Reilly & Britton, or the syndicate.

Meanwhile Reilly & Britton advertised *The Land of Oz* in major magazines and newspapers, distributed a special poster designed by Baum's new illustrator, John R. Neill, and published a song entitled "What Did the Woggle-Bug Say?" with words by Baum and music by Paul Tietjens, who had written music for the *Wizard of Oz* stage play. About the time that the

In addition to *The Woggle-Bug Book*, the newspaper contest, a Parker Brothers' Woggle-Bug game and a song, there were Woggle-Bug buttons, post cards and other giveaway items.

comic page began its run, Reilly & Britton sent out the first issue of a mock newspaper called The *Ozmapolitan,* filled with gossip about the latest events in Oz. Another *Ozmapolitan* appeared as a 1905 *Publishers Weekly* advertisement, and the same publicity device was used on later occasions through 1970.

In 1905 Baum published *The Woggle-Bug Book,* describing the adventures of that personage primarily in America, after he became separated from the other Queer Visitors. *The Woggle-Bug Book,* an oversize picture book with full-color illustrations by Ike Morgan on every page, is a disappointment after *The Marvelous Land of Oz,* but it sold well in its time.

All this activity was building up to the 1905 *Woggle-Bug* stage play (see page 129), which failed—a failure that served to emphasize the success of Baum's other Oz

activities during 1904 and 1905. No wonder that Denslow's claim to Oz made little impact on the public!

Baum was now at the most productive point in his career. While Reilly & Britton was shepherding *The Land* through the press, he was at work on two quite different fantasies. *Queen Zixi of Ix,* probably Baum's best non-Oz book, is a fairy tale closer to the traditional type than his previous work. It was serialized in *St. Nicholas* magazine and appeared in book form in 1905. Baum's nine *Animal Fairy Tales* were published in the *Delineator* magazine during 1905. Although the nine tales are somewhat uneven, on the whole they are excellent; it is surprising that they were not collected in book form until 1969.

In 1905 Baum also began to write for Reilly & Britton under various pseudonyms. These books were primarily series

Baum's 1906 fairy tale, *John Dough and the Cherub*, featured a contest on whether Chick, the cherub, was a boy or a girl.

for teen-agers, but they also included two adult romances, published under the name "Schuyler Staunton." With a few exceptions, Baum's pseudonymous books are hack work. The most popular of his teen-age series were those published under the name "Edith Van Dyne."

Baum's major fantasy for 1906 was *John Dough and the Cherub*, featuring John Dough, a live gingerbread man, and Chick the Cherub, the world's first incubator baby. To launch *John Dough*, the publishers worked out an elaborate—and today surprisingly contemporary—publicity contest to determine whether Chick was a boy or a girl. In 1907 came *Policeman Bluejay*, published under the pseudonym "Laura Bancroft" and later reprinted as *Babes in Birdland*.

A promotional leaflet for the third Oz book (above) and John R. Neill's poster, an adaptation of his drawing for the original dust jacket. (Courtesy Chicago Historical Society)

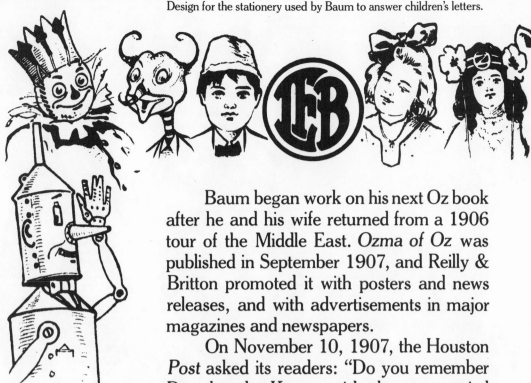

Design for the stationery used by Baum to answer children's letters.

Baum began work on his next Oz book after he and his wife returned from a 1906 tour of the Middle East. *Ozma of Oz* was published in September 1907, and Reilly & Britton promoted it with posters and news releases, and with advertisements in major magazines and newspapers.

On November 10, 1907, the Houston *Post* asked its readers: "Do you remember Dorothy, the Kansas girl who was carried to Oz by a cyclone? She did not appear in the second book. . . . Well, Mr. Baum's young admirers forced him into writing more about Dorothy. They sent him letters begging and pleading; they scolded and commanded, the Dorothys in real life being the most insistent of all. And so Mr. Baum sat himself down cheerfully . . . and made a new story about Dorothy and some old and new Ozzy creatures. He dedicated it to all the boys and girls who read his stories, 'especially the Dorothys.' " In fact, throughout his writing career Baum was extraordinarily responsive to the wishes of his young correspondents; he encouraged their letters in his prefaces, tried to answer all the children who wrote to him, and frequently wove their suggestions into his stories. The following letters from children were used in Reilly & Britton publicity. The spelling, punctuation and capitalization were reproduced scrupulously, but the dates were omitted.

Dear Mr. Baum: I just love the Wonderful Wizard of Oz. I have read it three times. My name is Dorothy too, and the Scarecrow and the Tin Woodman were so nice to Dorothy I would like very much to have you write another story about Dorothy and all of them. You don't have to make it very long, and of course you don't have to do it if you don't want to. We had a cyclone here once but I wasn't born. If I was born then, maybe I would have gone to the same place Dorothy did. I must close now.

With love from
Dorothy Hummer

New Milford Conn. Dear Sir could you make arrangements with Glinda the good Or Ozma to let the family and me make a visit to the land of Oz. and if there isn't any land of Oz let me know. the family and I would like to go as soon as possible. One reason I want to go to the land of Oz is because I want to get courage. Another reason is because I love adventure. I will pay for the wireless message.

truly yours,
William Beard

Surely the most gratifying of all the letters to Baum is the one quoted by Russell P. MacFall in *To Please a Child.* No signature is given:

I am going to write you a letter. You wrote a nice book. It's called *The Wizard of Oz.* I couldn't write a book like that. I think I love you.

In *Ozma of Oz,* Dorothy Gale and Uncle Henry (who is hardly the subsistence farmer of the first Oz book) are on their way to Australia to stay with cousins while he recovers his health. Dorothy and a chicken coop are blown overboard by a great storm, and she and a yellow hen are washed ashore in the Land of Ev, a fairyland separated from Oz by the Deadly Desert. Dorothy and the hen Billina discover Tik-Tok, a mechanical man, and then meet Ozma of Oz, who has crossed the Desert which surrounds Oz on a Magic Carpet together with the Scare-

OZMA OF OZ
L. FRANK BAUM

Jan 18 1907
Dear Mr Baum.
I wish to Write you
a letter. I thank
you y very Much.
I dont see how you
Could think up such
a nice storie

Your little friend
Charlotte Brenna

crow, the Tin Woodman, the Cowardly Lion, the Hungry Tiger, and the twenty-seven officers and one private of the Army of Oz. Ozma hopes to rescue the royal family of Ev from Roquat the Red, King of the Nomes, and Dorothy and her friends join them. After many adventures they return to Oz, where Ozma makes Dorothy a princess before she sends her by magic to her uncle in Australia.

Ozma of Oz is one of the finest of the Oz books; it adds important new characters and develops important new themes. Tik-Tok (a mechanical man manufactured by the Evian firm of Smith & Tinker), who can do anything but live, is a permanent addition to the Oz pantheon, as are the yellow hen Billina and the Hungry Tiger, whose conscience won't let him eat fat babies. The best new character, however, is the Nome King (Baum thought that "Gnome" was too difficult a word for his readers to pronounce), and the most complex of the themes centers on his great fear of eggs. Roquat is Machiavellian: he pretends to be friendly to further his own desires. As with most Machiavellians, his plotting causes his own downfall, when the yellow hen overhears him. Baum is never quite clear what sort of poison eggs are to the Nomes, but symbolically, Roquat and his men are terrified of eggs because they represent life and fertility.

Although Baum wanted to write other sorts of fantasies by this time—perhaps even before the publication of *Ozma*—he complied with his publisher's request that he provide an Oz book a year for the next few years at least. Good as Baum's other fantasies were, they did not sell like the Oz books.

The next two Oz books, unfortunately, are poorer than the first three, perhaps because Baum was spending more energy on

Princess Languidere of Ev, the lady with thirty heads. Neill's drawing is a skillful parody of the Gibson girl.

BY THE AID OF THE MIRROR SHE PUT ON THE HEAD

"THIS COPPER MAN IS NOT ALIVE AT ALL"

various stage projects, most of which were unproduced; the exception was the play *Ozma of Oz*, written around 1908–9 and produced in 1913 as *The Tik-Tok Man of Oz* (see pages 139 ff.).

Dorothy and the Wizard in Oz, the 1908 Oz book, is the shortest of Baum's Oz titles and shows signs of having been written quickly. Since bringing Dorothy back in *Ozma of Oz* had been successful, Baum decided in the next Oz book to bring back the Wizard himself, apparently forgetting (as most readers have also proved willing to do) that the Wizard had been revealed as something of a villain at the end of *The Marvelous Land of Oz*. Dorothy, her cat Eureka, a young boy named Zeb, his old horse Jim, the Wizard, and his nine tiny piglets are

caught by a California earthquake and journey underground toward Oz. Eventually, they are rescued by Ozma and then spend too much of the book in an Oz less interesting than their underground journey. At the end of the book, the Wizard accepts Ozma's offer of a home. *Dorothy and the Wizard in Oz* is a tale of gloom, bravery and frustration. It has been criticized because it is so gloomy, but children can take that better than some adults. *Dorothy and the Wizard* is, in fact, a fascinating failure.

The reviewers greeted *Dorothy and the Wizard* cordially, referring to Oz, after eight years and four books, as a "perennial favorite." In fact, the tradition of a new Oz book for Christmas, which is part of the memories

L. FRANK BAUM telling "OZ" stories at Coronado

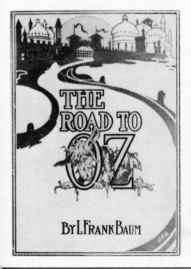

THE ROAD TO OZ

BY L. FRANK BAUM

DOROTHY AND THE WIZARD IN OZ

BY L. FRANK BAUM

of thousands of American families, was already established.

The 1909 title, *The Road to Oz*, is the poorest Baum book in the series. The plot, which quickly becomes tedious, reveals how Dorothy, Toto and a wandering tramp called the Shaggy Man follow a road into fairyland. On their journey they are joined by Button-Bright, a little boy who is lost, and Polychrome, the daughter of the Rainbow. In the end it turns out that Ozma confused the roads so that Dorothy could come to her birthday party. After the celebration, which is described at some length, Dorothy returns home.

The Road to Oz is interesting primarily for its new characters. Polychrome, Button-Bright and the Shaggy Man (a romanticized tramp based upon James Whitcomb Riley's Raggedy Man) become permanent fixtures in later Oz books. And at the end Baum ties almost all his fairy tales together by having Queen Zixi, John Dough, Chick the Cherub, Santa Claus, the Queen of

An original drawing by Neill for *The Road to Oz*. Neill's early Oz illustrations were extremely elaborate and filled with flights of fancy. Notice that one Scoodler has a pawnbroker's sign for a nose, two have monetary systems and one has a tiny cannon on its head.

Original drawing for *The Road to Oz.*

The cover of the first edition of *The Emerald City of Oz.*

Merryland and other characters from his non-Oz books attend Ozma's birthday party.

In his preface to *Dorothy and the Wizard,* Baum had indicated that he wanted to write fantasies not about Oz, but the children wouldn't let him; in his preface to *The Road to Oz* he warned that the next volume might be the last in the series. He was tired of his creation. The economics of book publishing limited him to one major children's fantasy a year, and as long as the Oz series went on, that fantasy had to be an Oz book. He had on hand two major un-published books—*Animal Fairy Tales* and *King Rinkitink*—and he was toying with an idea for a new series about a little girl and an old sailor. So he decided to end the Oz series with the 1910 title, *The Emerald City of Oz.*

The *Emerald City* has two plots, which alternate throughout the book, one dealing with Dorothy and her family and friends, and the other with the machinations of the Nome King, who decides to conquer Oz. Dorothy's Uncle Henry and Aunt Em are about to lose their farm because they cannot pay the mortgage. When Dorothy makes a sign, Ozma transports her to the Emerald City and agrees to allow her and her relatives to make their homes permanently in Oz. After Uncle Henry and Aunt Em are magically transported to Oz and recover from their surprise, Dorothy and the Wizard take them on a grand tour of the country. After many adventures they learn from the Tin Woodman that Ozma has found out that the Nome King and a great army are tunneling under the Deadly Desert to invade Oz; but she is unwilling to fight even to save the country, thus carrying pacifism to a level possible only in a fairyland. They return to the Emerald City, where all seems lost until the Scarecrow suggests that they make use of the Forbidden Fountain, containing the Water of Oblivion, which makes everyone who drinks it forget all he has ever known. By magic, Ozma fills the tunnel with dust. When the invaders emerge they are so thirsty that they drink immediately. All that remains is for the now-childish Roquat to march his Nomes back through the tunnel, which is then closed up. To prevent other enemies from invading Oz, Glinda surrounds the entire country with a barrier of invisibility. The book ends with a note from Dorothy advising Baum that because of the barrier there can be no more stories about Oz.

Reilly & Britton placed advertisements all over the country for "The Last of the 'Oz' Books," stating that *The Emerald City* "is the most beautiful" of the series and "assembles more characters than possibly any other children's book contains." Unless one counts all the soldiers in Roquat's invading armies, the latter claim is certainly false (*Alice in Wonderland,* for one, "assembles" more); the former is entirely correct. Sixteen illustrations by Neill, as well as the front-cover label, were printed in full color, including metallic green, and the spine was embellished with silver. The color plates were all taken from paintings, beautifully reproduced and engraved.

The Emerald City was favorably reviewed, although comments were sometimes perfunctory; the annual addition to the Oz canon was no longer especially newsworthy. Several reviewers speculated that Oz would not end with the sixth book. The Portland (Oregon) *Telegram* for October 22, 1910, spoke for the vast Oz readership: "Children have been told about the beautiful Land of Bonbon, of the clime where the rainbow is born, of the haunts of the Brownies, but these fairy nations are not Oz, and the children want it. The only graceful way Baum can quit telling tales of Oz is to die."

In the two years before *The Emerald City* was published, Baum's financial affairs had again become seriously entangled. In

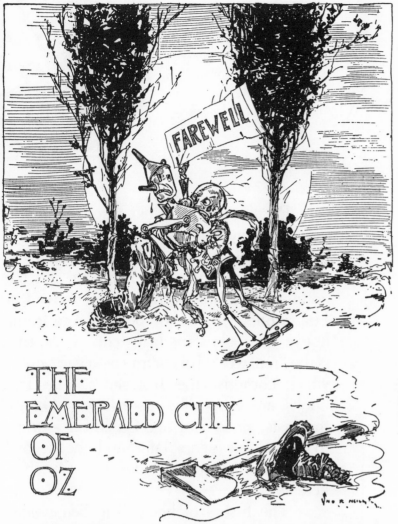

How **THEY DRANK AT THE FORBIDDEN FOUNTAIN**

CHAPTER TWENTY-EIGHT

How **THE SCARECROW DISPLAYED HIS WISDOM**

Probably The Wisest Man in All Oz.

CHAPTER TWENTY-FIVE

The title page and some chapter headings for *The Emerald City of Oz*, intended by Baum to be "the last of the Oz books."

1908 he produced his *Fairylogue and Radio-Plays* (see page 131). Although it was well received, it was not well financed, and it left Baum with heavy debts. He was forced in 1909 to contract with Reilly & Britton for a monthly salary based upon his previous year's royalties. In 1910 his monetary problems had become so acute that he assigned all rights in his Bobbs-Merrill books to a group of creditors. This agreement included the rights to *The Wizard of Oz* itself, rights that were not regained by Baum's widow until 1932. Drastic as the sacrifice was, it did not long ward off a greater crisis, for in June 1911, L. Frank Baum declared bankruptcy. There was considerable newspaper publicity.

How **THE STORY OF OZ CAME TO AN END**

CHAPTER THIRTY

Baum, who never lost his love for grease paint and footlights, appeared in a 1914 production of The Uplifters, a Los Angeles social group.

At this glad time of Holiday
When greetings fond are due.
I hope your thoughts will turn my way
As mine have turned to you.

L. Frank Baum

A Christmas card from Ozcot.

Partly to cut their expenses and partly because they had fallen in love with California, Frank and Maud Baum had in 1910 given up their home in Chicago and the cottage on Lake Michigan and moved to Hollywood, where they built a large frame house they christened "Ozcot." California is the "real world" of Baum's next two books, which comprise the Trot series. The Trot books are especially interesting to Oz enthusiasts, since Trot and Cap'n Bill journey to Oz a few years later and the second book, *Sky Island*, includes two Oz characters.

The first Trot book, *The Sea Fairies* (1911), describes the adventures among the mermaids of Trot (her real name is Mayre Griffiths), a little California girl, and her constant companion, Cap'n Bill Weedles, a grizzled old sailor with a wooden leg. *Sky Island* (1912) takes Trot, Cap'n Bill and our old friend Button-Bright to an island in the sky where they meet Polychrome, another friend from the Oz books.

The two Trot books are illustrated by John R. Neill, and Reilly & Britton was careful to make them look as much like Oz books as possible. Baum expected to continue the series with a new book each year, but the verdict of the buying public came quickly: *The Sea Fairies* sold 12,401 copies during 1911, while *The Emerald City of Oz* had sold about 20,000 copies in its first year. This distressing fact, plus Baum's bankruptcy and an overwhelming number of letters from children asking for "more about

The cover design for *The Patchwork Girl of Oz* and the cutout figure by Neill distributed by the publishers to advertise the book.

The Patchwork Girl of Oz

Dorothy," led to a decision by author and publisher even before *Sky Island* appeared. Cutting off contact with Oz had brought a reaction second only to that following Sherlock Holmes's death at Reichenbach Falls, and Baum's readers rejoiced when *The Patchwork Girl of Oz* appeared in 1913. Baum was fated to remain Royal Historian of Oz (as he now called himself) for the rest of his life.

The *Patchwork Girl of Oz* is the first really excellent Oz book after *Ozma of Oz*. Baum's preface informs his readers that contact with Oz has been re-established by wireless telegraph. The story that comes over the wireless is that of Ojo, a young Munchkin boy, as he searches for the ingredients needed to break the enchantments of his Unk Nunkie and Margolotte, who have been accidentally transformed into marble statues by a potion belonging to Margolotte's husband, the crooked magician Dr. Pipt. Ojo is accompanied in his quest by a glass cat named Bungle and by Scraps, a girl made from a patchwork quilt. They are joined by the Woozy, a square beast

Victor Columbia Edison.

The Woozy.

whose three tail hairs are necessary ingredients for the magic compound of disenchantment, and by the Shaggy Man, who rescues them from man-eating plants. When they reach the Emerald City, Ojo sees another ingredient, a six-leaf clover, and picks it even though he knows that this is against the law. He is arrested, spends a night in a pleasant jail and is forgiven by Ozma.

A new party—Ojo, Scraps, Dorothy, Toto and the Scarecrow—sets out to find the other items necessary for the magic compound. Eventually they obtain all the ingredients except the left wing of a yellow butterfly, which they confidently expect the Tin Woodman, emperor of the yellow country of the Winkies, to help them find. He, however, is horrified and refuses to allow them to maim a single butterfly. They return sorrowfully to the Emerald City, where the Wizard, with a magic pass he has learned from Glinda, disenchants Unk Nunkie and Margolotte.

The Patchwork Girl of Oz tells how Ojo matures. He learns about honesty and punishment—and ultimately that nothing,

not even restoring his uncle, justifies cruelty to a living creature.

Baum's amazing facility in creating grotesques was never greater than in *Patchwork Girl*: Victor Columbia Edison, a living phonograph named after the chief manufacturers of talking machines; the Glass Cat, transparent except for her ruby heart and pink brains ("You can see 'em work"); the square Woozy, a living parody of cubist paintings; Unk Nunkie, who speaks in as few monosyllables as possible—to name only a few. The greatest of them, and one of the great American fantasy characters, is Scraps the Patchwork Girl, fashioned by Margolotte to be a servant and brought to life by Dr. Pipt's Powder of Life, the same powder used in *The Marvelous Land of Oz*.

Beginning with *The Patchwork Girl of Oz*, we have occasional insights into how Baum worked, based on his correspondence with his publishers. On January 23, 1912, he wrote to S. C. Britton:

A lot of thought is required on one of these fairy tales. The odd characters are a sort of inspiration, liable to strike me any time, but the plot and plan of adventures take considerable time to develop. When I get at a thing of that sort I live with it day by day, jotting down on odd slips of paper the various ideas that occur and in this way getting my material together. The new Oz book [*Patchwork Girl*] is in this stage. I've got it all—all the hard work has been done—and it's a dandy I think. But laws-a-massy! it's a long way from being ready for the printer yet. I must rewrite it, stringing the incidents into consecutive order, elaborating the characters, etc. Then it's typewritten. Then it's revised, retypewritten and sent on to Reilly & Britton.

Reilly & Britton sprang *The Patchwork Girl* on an unsuspecting public and

---

The Ozmapolitan

EMERALD CITY—LAND OF OZ

No. X3Z   5TH DAY –3RD PERIOD–REIGN OF OZMA   VOL. Q

A SWELL DINNER

The Mayor of Jupiter to Entertain Distinguished Visitors from Land of Oz.

Jupiter, 4th day, 3rd period. (Wireless special to OZMAPOLITAN.) Arrangements are being made by the Mayor of this Orb to entertain the Scarecrow and Tin Woodman party as they come through on their way to the United States in August. It is most likely that the celebration will take the form of an Air-ship Banquet, and the government armored air cruiser "Constellation" will probably be redecorated in Royal Green and Gold, emblematic of the Land of Oz, as a mark of special courtesy toward the representatives of Her Royal Highness, Princess Ozma of Oz.

It is also expected that the Mayor will proclaim the day of the Banquet a National Holiday.

FAREWELL TO JINJUR.

A handshaking was given last night in honor of ex-General Jinjur, late of the army of revolt, at which many of her sympathizers were on hand to give her public

Jinjur

notice of their constancy to her cause. They feel that when her personal memoirs are written and disseminated among the people there will come into the public mind a new view of the causes leading to the revolt. Whether or not she succeeds in justifying her cause it may be truthfully said that the General is very popular and minus her extreme political tendencies would be in line for highest honors. It was noticed that many attended the function who were thought to be unalterably opposed to her ideas.

YIELDS CONSENT.

THE SCARECROW MAY GO.

The Princess Decides that the Trip to the United States May be Made.

After many consultations and the sending of many wireless specials to the United States, Her Royal Majesty, the Princess Ozma, has at last consented to the proposed visit of the Scarecrow and the Tin Woodman to the United States. Mr. L. Frank Baum and Mr. Walt McDougall has promised to give them a good time and see that no harm comes to them. It is said that a million children want to see them in that faraway country owing to the kindly story written of them by Mr. Baum, our official historian. However, it was not until Little Dorothy of Kansas sent her special plea that the Princess finally gave her consent. Little Dorothy says she may return with them, and if she does it is needless to say she will be royally received. She says Toto, her very intelligent dog, is well and will come with her.

A GREAT DISCOVERY

University of Mars Experiments may Revolutionize Transmission of News.

MARS, 4th day, 3rd period. (Special wireless aerogram to the OZMAPOLITAN.) The astrological department of the University of Mars has determined to test the value of their new signal method of communication with other worlds, and accordingly will try to arrange with the Scarecrow and Tin Woodman party to make observations and note what points they are able to see the signals. The result of this experiment will be watched with great interest as the new method is much less expensive than the present wireless system of communication by electricity.

See Large Advertisement on Page 4.

EXCURSIONS TO ST. LOUIS

The Interplanetary Company May Undertake to Blaze a Trail to Big Exhibition.

The Flying Machine business seems to be in a most flourishing condition, all of the manufacturers reporting more orders than they can fill. The Zerchou - Eddisonne Machine comes on the market within a short time. These will be of the large excursion aeromobile pattern and will be put in service by the Interplanetary Co., Ltd.

Mr. Zerchou desires to make a trial voyage to America, going over the same route as the Scarecrow party. He says he can make the voyage in one-third less time than the Flying Gump, and with twenty people on board. So confident is he of this notion that he is willing to make a rate of forty pequots per passenger for the round trip, allowing a reasonable stay in the faraway land. He hopes to bring about this excursion in time to visit the great St. Louis Exposition before it closes.

RETURNED WITH THANKS

Whether he did it as a joke or not, a New York architect has caused a lot of fun among the officials of our city. Having heard that a valuable prize had been offered for the best plan for relieving the congestion of the city's population, this architect sent plans for a huge building four stories high, each floor constituting a complete home in itself. In this manner the same ground would be sufficient to accommodate four families. The architect said that these apartments were called "flats" in New York and Chicago.

The Scarecrow on being shown the building and the plans laughed heartily and said: "That reminds me of the stories I have read about the Cliff Dwellers. As for myself, I would not like to live in a house where I could not fail to the grass without hurting myself."

Not wishing to offend the architect the officials returned the plans with the statement that the people of the Land of Oz preferred not to be housed in stacks. When they want to go home they do not care to be hauled up with a rope.

WILL LEAVE SOON.

FOR THE UNITED STATES.

The Scarecrow Submits to an Interesting Interview Concerning the Proposed Trip to America.

The Scarecrow was seen last night regarding his trip to the United States. He was very much pleased that Royal consent has been

(LATEST PORTRAIT OF THE SCARECROW, By NEIL.)

given, and submitted to the following interview:

"We will start," said he, "about the first of August and will expect to land somewhere on American soil early in September."

"Where will you land," was asked?

"It is impossible to say. It all depends on the air currents we strike as we approach the earth. It is expected that L. Frank Baum and Walt McDougall, the artist, will meet us wherever we effect a landing. We shall head for a place called 'Philadelphia,' but by the use of powerful telescopes our hosts can tell about where we will land and reach us by what they call 'railroads.'"

"Is your party fully made up?"

"Yes, it is. There will be on board the Flying Gump, H. M. Woggle-Bug, T. E., Jack Pumpkinhead, Nick Chopper, the Tin Woodman, and myself. That loads the Gump to the guard rails. We really should not take the Saw Horse along, but Jack refuses to come without his noble steed. I don't know but what he is right, as the Saw Horse is likely to be

Concluded on page 3, 3d column.

promoted it for all it was worth (which was quite a bit). Sales were substantially better than those of the Trot books, although they did not reach the first-year totals of the earlier Oz titles. (Sales of new Oz books did not reach the earlier records until about 1918 or 1919.)

As part of the promotion, Reilly & Britton published six Oz stories by Baum in 1913 that have remained little known even to most Oz enthusiasts. These "Oz books in Miniature" (as an advertisement called them) comprise The Little Wizard Series. Each is an original twenty-nine-page story with textual illustrations by John R. Neill in color and in blue (because the text is printed in blue ink rather than black) and full-color cover designs. The original booklets are similar in format to Little Golden Books. In 1914 they were reissued as a single volume, Little Wizard Stories of Oz; in 1932 four of the stories were reprinted as The Little Oz Books with Jig Saw Oz Puzzles; in 1933 or 1934 the same four were reprinted as premiums for the Jell-O Wizard of Oz radio program; and in 1939 Rand McNally reprinted all six stories in three booklets.

The stories are, on the whole, very good. The Cowardly Lion and the Hungry Tiger describes how the two great beasts go into the streets of the Emerald City seeking a fat baby for the Tiger to devour and a grownup for the Lion to tear to pieces; instead, they find a lost child and return him to his mother. Little Dorothy and Toto tells of the kidnapping of Dorothy and her dog by the giant Crinklink, who turns out to be the Wizard trying to teach them that it is "dangerous to wander alone in a fairy country." Tiktok and the Nome King, probably the best of the series, describes Tik-Tok's mission to the metal monarch. Tik-Tok angers the Nome King by "a true, yet an unwise speech" ("I'm not a-fraid of a fat

The Ork, from *The Scarecrow of Oz.*

Nome"), and the furious king tears the clockwork man to pieces. Fortunately, his steward Kaliko manages to reassemble Tik-Tok, and for a few hilarious minutes the Nome King thinks he is confronted by a ghost: "Look out! Here comes a phantom clockwork man!" *Ozma and the Little Wizard,* a much tamer story, tells how the two try to vanquish three imps, who manage to remain mischievous in every form they are transformed into except buttons. *In Jack Pumpkinhead and the Sawhorse,* the title characters go on a deed of mercy into a forest to rescue two children who have been captured by squirrels. *The Scarecrow and the Tin Woodman* is the last and least of the stories. It tells how the two old friends meet various calamities while out for a peaceful boat ride on a river.

The year 1913 was a busy one for Baum and Oz; it saw not only the publication of *The Patchwork Girl of Oz* and The Little Wizard Series, but also the produc-

Button Bright and the Bumpy Man, from *The Scarecrow of Oz.*

tion of Baum's "musical extravaganza," *The Tik-Tok Man of Oz* (see page 141) which became the basis of the book *Tik-Tok of Oz*, the 1914 addition to the Oz canon.

Since *The Tik-Tok Man* play began as Baum's 1908–9 dramatization of *Ozma of Oz*, reading the 1914 Oz book can give one a sense of *déjà vu*. The heroine, Betsy Bobbin, is a girl from Oklahoma. Like Dorothy in the earlier book, she is blown off a ship and floats to shore—not, however, with a yellow hen but with a mule named Hank. They land in the Rose Country, a coastal enclave in Ev, meet Tik-Tok and other Oz characters, join forces with Queen Ann of Oogaboo, who is out to conquer the world, and tangle with the Nome King, who has relearned his wickedness but forgotten his original name and taken another: Ruggedo. In the end the travelers are trans-

ported to Oz, where Betsy and Hank become permanent residents.

Tik-Tok of Oz is interesting for its themes. As in *Ozma of Oz*, the Nome King is defeated by eggs, and the Nomes turn another symbol of life and growth into the beautiful but sterile Metal Forest. War, the greatest of all destructive forces, is made much more ridiculous than it was in *Ozma of Oz*. Unlike many commentators of his time, Baum recognized that war is dehumanizing. But the greatest addition to our knowledge of Oz in Tik-Tok is the end-

August 28, 1915   *The Publishers' Weekly*   595

Following the precedent of other years and other Oz Books

The Scarecrow of Oz

By L. Frank Baum

will be The Leading Juvenile for 1915

"My best," says the author. John R. Neill has certainly played up to that estimate in his illustrations. His fertile imagination and keen sense of whimsy and fun have created some droll and delightful pictures—over a hundred, 12 of them in full color. Medallion chapter heads; tailpieces, special decorations galore; color endsheets.

The Scarecrow has always been a favorite character; now he has the center of the stage, but the background is crowded with the drollest of Baum creations. The "Ork" alone is worth a whole book. Captivating adventures, humor and fun; Cap'n Bill, Tiny Trot, Button Bright, Dorothy and Betsy Bobbin, always hailed with delight, are all there.

Our window display material is very fetching. It includes a cut-out, 32 inches high, in colors, of the Scarecrow.

Uniform with the other Oz Books. Striking display jacket and cover in full color. $1.25.

paper maps of Oz and the countries surrounding it (see page 44), which were printed in full color.

By the end of 1914, Baum had nearly completed *The Scarecrow of Oz*. Although author and publisher had been displeased with the sales of *Tik-Tok*, they knew that it, like the other Oz titles, would sell steadily in succeeding years, while there had been little market for the two Trot books beyond their first year. But Baum liked Trot and Cap'n Bill, so he decided to bring them to Oz in *The Scarecrow*.

The little girl and the old seaman begin this adventure when they are sucked down by a whirlpool to a cavern deep under the ocean. There they are joined by another whirlpool victim, the Ork—a bird with four wings, four legs and a propeller tail—with whom they escape. Later they again meet Button-Bright, and eventually, of course, reach Oz, where they defeat the wicked King of Jinxland and are finally offered a home in the Emerald City.

The Scarecrow is not a bad book, and it was Baum's own favorite among his Oz titles. Like *Tik-Tok of Oz*, it is partially based on a dramatization, this time on a screenplay, *His Majesty, The Scarecrow of Oz* (see page 149). Most of Baum's energies during 1914 were expended on his Oz Film Manufacturing Company, which he had founded to make silent movies of his books. The firm collapsed after completing five features and a few shorts, but this time Baum had not invested his own funds and was not hurt financially.

Because sales for *Tik-Tok* had been disappointing, Reilly & Britton began a major sales campaign in 1915, advertising *The Scarecrow* heavily and distributing posters, cutout figures and celluloid buttons. The most elaborate publicity device was *The Oz Toy Book, Cut-outs for the Kiddies*, a sixteen-page collection of full-color cutouts by

Neill's cover for the now rare *Oz Toy Book* (1914). Cutouts from the book appear on the next two pages.

Wizard

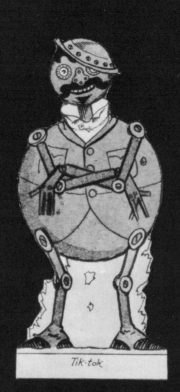

Tik-tok

Ozma

Scarecrow

Jack Pumpkinhead

Tin Woodman

Dorothy

Hungry Tiger

Cowardly Lion

I M P A S S A B L

GILL

COU

MOUNTAIN

MT. MUNCH

MUNCHKIN

Jinjur's House

Munchkin

COUNTRY

ERA

Where Dorothy's House Fell

Road of Yellow Brick

River

Poppy Field

College of Prof. Wogglebug

Miss Cuttenclip

Forest

Fuddlecu

QUADLING

DICKSY

Ojo's House

F O R E S T

POOL

Magic Waterfall

Palace of Glinda the Go

JINXLAND

G R E A T   S A

S H I F T I N G   S A N D S

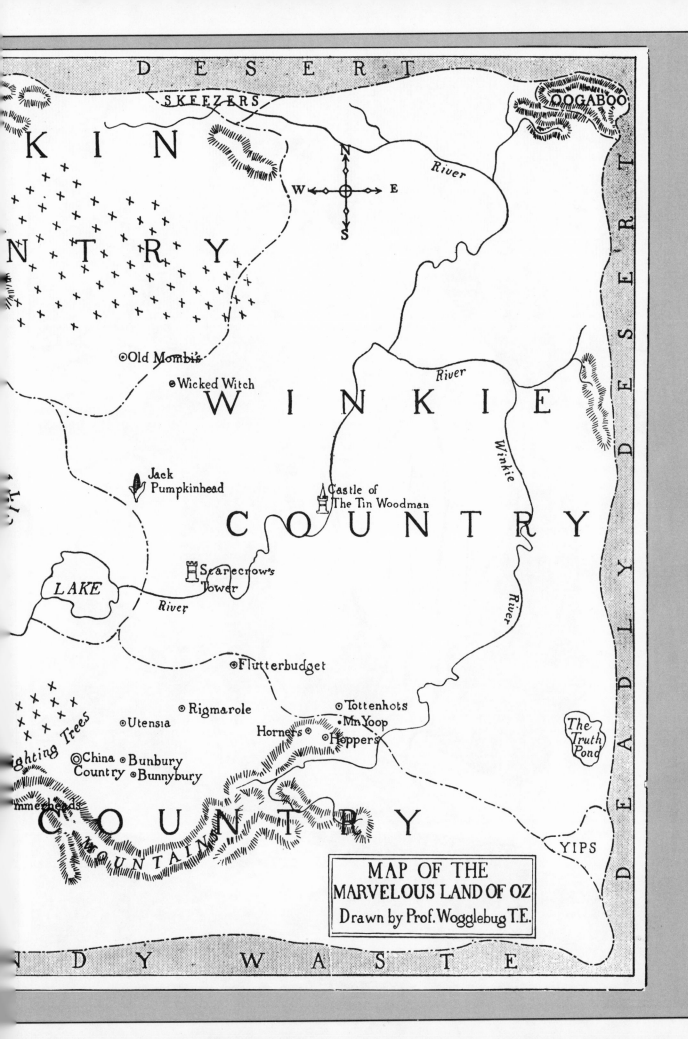

MAP OF THE
MARVELOUS LAND OF OZ
Drawn by Prof. Wogglebug T.E.

King
Rinkitink.

John Neill of the Oz characters. Although it was primarily an advertising gimmick, the publisher thought so highly of Neill's drawings that it decided to market the booklet—and neglected to mention the project to Baum, who learned of it only when he received a Reilly & Britton catalogue. Baum rightly believed that some of his problems with Denslow had been the result of Denslow's holding the copyright for his *Wizard* drawings; and he had decided that he would never again allow an illustrator to retain rights to the drawings of Baum characters. Hence he exploded. F. K. Reilly belatedly explained what the publisher had done, pointed out that *The Oz Toy Book* was manufactured so flimsily that it would fall apart with any real usage, and apologized profusely. Baum graciously accepted the apology, and the crisis was over.

For some time, however, Baum had been concerned about Neill's illustrations for the Oz books, and the problems over *The Oz Toy Book,* which Baum thought unattractive, made him want to find another artist. Part of Baum's concern can probably be traced back to the fact that with Denslow he had had a personal relationship, while his connection with Neill was almost entirely through the publisher. Whatever the cause, Baum did not think Neill's fine line work humorous enough for his audience, and he suggested that Reilly & Britton try someone like the cartoonist George McManus, creator of *Bringing Up Father,* or Winsor McKay, famed *for Little*

Nemo. The publisher was well satisfied with Neill, and fortunately Baum did not press the issue; his later Oz books do not look like Sunday comic pages. Baum was, of course, wrong; without Neill's drawings, Oz would be a poorer place.

For his next Oz book, Baum decided to use his unpublished manuscript *King Rinkitink,* which appeared in 1916 as *Rinkitink in Oz.* Rinkitink is essentially the story of Prince Inga of Pingaree, an island in the Nonestic Ocean, which surrounds the continent on which Baum placed most of his fairylands. Inga, with the help of three magic pearls, fat King Rinkitink of a neighboring kingdom, and Rinkitink's talking goat Bilbil, sets out to rescue his parents and the other islanders, all of whom have been carried off into slavery by marauders.

The book leaves one with a sense of pleasure that Baum found a way of publishing such a fine fantasy, and disappointment that he had to pull Dorothy into it at the end and conclude the book in the Emerald City. Why, most readers have asked themselves, couldn't Inga, who does so much, ultimately free his parents? In the original manuscript, he probably did.

After the failure of his Oz Film Manufacturing Company, Baum was involved in very few creative projects other than the Oz series and his annual teen-age book by "Edith Van Dyne." He was growing old, and his health, which had been uncertain since his childhood, was becoming increasingly worrisome. By 1917 he was suffering

from gall-bladder attacks. Because he could not take on so many projects as before, he was able to concentrate on Oz, and his final four Oz books, none based on an earlier manuscript or drama, are, with the possible exception of *The Tin Woodman of Oz*, among the best in the long series. Sales, which began increasing in 1916, continued to climb steadily.

Baum began planning *The Lost Princess of Oz*, which appeared in 1917, two years earlier. His first title was *Three Girls in Oz*, and the book was originally to be the adventures of Dorothy, Betsy Bobbin and Trot. The final plot, however, is that of a mystery story. The tone is set by the striking opening: "There could be no doubt of the fact: Princess Ozma, the lovely girl ruler of the Fairyland of Oz, was lost. She had completely disappeared. Not one of her subjects—not even her closest friends—knew what had become of her." Not only had Ozma disappeared but almost all the important instruments of Oz magic had gone also: Glinda's Great Book of Records, the Wizard's Black Bag of magic, Ozma's Magic Picture. All the famous inhabitants of Oz are organized into three search parties to seek Ozma throughout the country. Most of the book centers on the party headed by the Wizard and Dorothy. They finally confront the powerful magician Ugu the Shoemaker, who has kidnapped Ozma. Dorothy turns him into a dove, and Ozma is discovered imprisoned in a peach pit.

The Lost Princess of Oz is a satisfying Oz mystery, with interesting characters and

The Frogman.

well-developed suspense. The giant Frog-man, who turns up on the search for Ozma, is yet another notable addition to the gallery of grotesques. Like the Woggle-Bug, he has grown to the size of a man, and also like the Woggle-Bug, his great size makes him pretend to wisdom he doesn't possess. Ugu is one of Baum's best villains. He possesses a drive for power with which the reader is forced to sympathize. The end of the book is particularly satisfying: Ugu repents his wickedness and decides to remain a dove.

The Tin Woodman of Oz (1918) poses another Oz puzzle, though hardly one so serious as the disappearance of Ozma. The Tin Woodman, Nick Chopper, tells the story of how he became tin to the latest Baum hero, a young boy called Woot the Wanderer. Woot asks Nick why he didn't return to marry the young Munchkin girl (whose name we learn is Nimmie Amee) after he had obtained his heart. When the Tin Woodman replies that he was given a kind heart, not a loving heart, Woot accuses him, justifiably though impertinently, of unkindness in not returning to Nimmie Amee. Nick, the Scarecrow and Woot set out to find the girl so she can become the Tin Woodman's empress. Eventually they meet Captain Fyter, the Tin Soldier, who became tin in exactly the same way as Nick and for the love of the same girl. Captain Fyter joins the group, and he and the Tin Woodman agree that Nimmie Amee shall choose between them. When they find the girl's house long abandoned, they visit Ku-Klip, the tin-

smith who manufactured both of them. He
is unable to help them with their quest, but
he does tell them of Chopfyt, a man he assembled, à la Dr. Frankenstein, out of the
human pieces of the two tin men. When they
finally track down the missing girl, they find
she is married to Chopfyt.

The Tin Woodman centers on questions of identity. Who is Chopfyt? How are
he and his two donors related to each other?
What is the relationship between Nick and
his severed human head, with which he holds
a conversation in Ku-Klip's workshop? Neither tin man has ever questioned his own
identity before; now they are forced to do so.
It is a humbling experience.

Despite its provocative theme, which
Thomas Mann explored much later, *The
Tin Woodman* is the most flawed of Baum's
later Oz books. Much of it is spent in an
episodic tour of Oz, without any real connection with the quest and without any particularly interesting episodes or characters.

In February 1918 Baum entered the
hospital to have his gall bladder removed.
Just before he went, he wrote his publisher
that he had "finished the *second* Oz book—
beyond the 'Tin Woodman of Oz'—which
will give you a manuscript for 1919 and
1920. Also there is material for another
book, so in case anything happens to me the
Baum books can be issued until and including 1921."

The Magic of Oz and *Glinda of Oz*, the
two books Baum had completed before his
operation, mark an important change in

Ugu the Shoemaker

Trot and Cap'n Bill take root in *The Magic of Oz*.

the series. They are more somber than any other Oz title except *Dorothy and the Wizard in Oz*.

   The Magic of Oz was published in 1919, just after Reilly & Britton had changed its name to Reilly & Lee. Like *The Emerald City*, it has two contrasting plots. The primary one deals with Kiki Aru, a most unpleasant Munchkin lad, and Ruggedo, the deposed Nome King. Kiki learns Pyrzqxgl, a magic word of transformation that works only when it is pronounced correctly. He changes himself into a hawk and flies away to the Land of Ev, where he meets the Nome

An adaptation of the end paper design from *Glinda of Oz*, used in an advertisement for an Oz Festival at Gimbel Brothers' department store in Philadelphia the year following Baum's death, one of thousands of Oz celebrations held during Baum's lifetime and in the almost sixty years since.

The Li-Mon-Eags (*The Magic of Oz*).

King who convinces him that they can conquer Oz. As eagles they fly back across the Deadly Desert to enlist the beasts of Oz as their allies. Under their next transformations as Li-Mon-Eags (they have "the heads of lions, the bodies of monkeys, the wings of eagles and the tails of wild asses"), they convince the animals in the Gillikin Forest that the people of Oz are about to enslave them unless they arise first. Meanwhile the unsuspecting Ozians are preparing for Ozma's birthday party. Dorothy and the Wizard decide to go to the Gillikin forests to find monkeys that they can train to jump out of

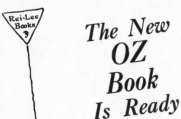

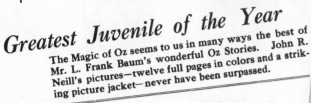

the birthday cake. They arrive just as the Nome King is exhorting the animals to overthrow their oppressors. After being themselves transformed into animals, Dorothy and the Wizard regain their own shapes and transform the two conspirators into a walnut and a hickory nut. Ozma's birthday is a great success; the walnut and the hickory nut are disenchanted and drink the Water of Oblivion.

The Magic of Oz is an important book for several reasons. As C. Warren Hollister has suggested, the revolt of the animals is probably a parody of the Russian Revolution, which had occurred two years before the book was published. (Surely the animals will revolt again if they are asked to jump out of too many cakes.) Trot and Cap'n Bill, who literally take root on an enchanted island where they have gone to get Ozma a magic plant, and start to shrink, face the most frightening fate in all the Baum Oz books. By being lured nearly to destruction by beauty, they place *The Magic of Oz* in one

In 1901, four years after Baum's first children's book was published,
the George M. Hill Company issued this poster, reflecting his extraordinary output.
(Courtesy Chicago Historical Society)

Wallpaper designs by W.W. Denslow (circa 1903) showing the characters as they appeared in the musical *The Wizard of Oz.*

Color illustrations from the original edition of, above, *The Wonderful Wizard of Oz* (1900) and, below, *The Marvelous Land of Oz* (1904).

The original dust jacket for *The Road to Oz* (1909).

The end pages in the original edition of *Ozma of Oz* (1907). A contemporary reviewer commented that it "appears to be a

circus race gone mad."

"I'M THE COOK".

Two original water-color paintings by John R. Neill for *The Emerald City of Oz* (1910).

The paper dolls and snippets surrounding Miss Cuttenclip are actual cut-outs pasted to the painting, an early example of collage.

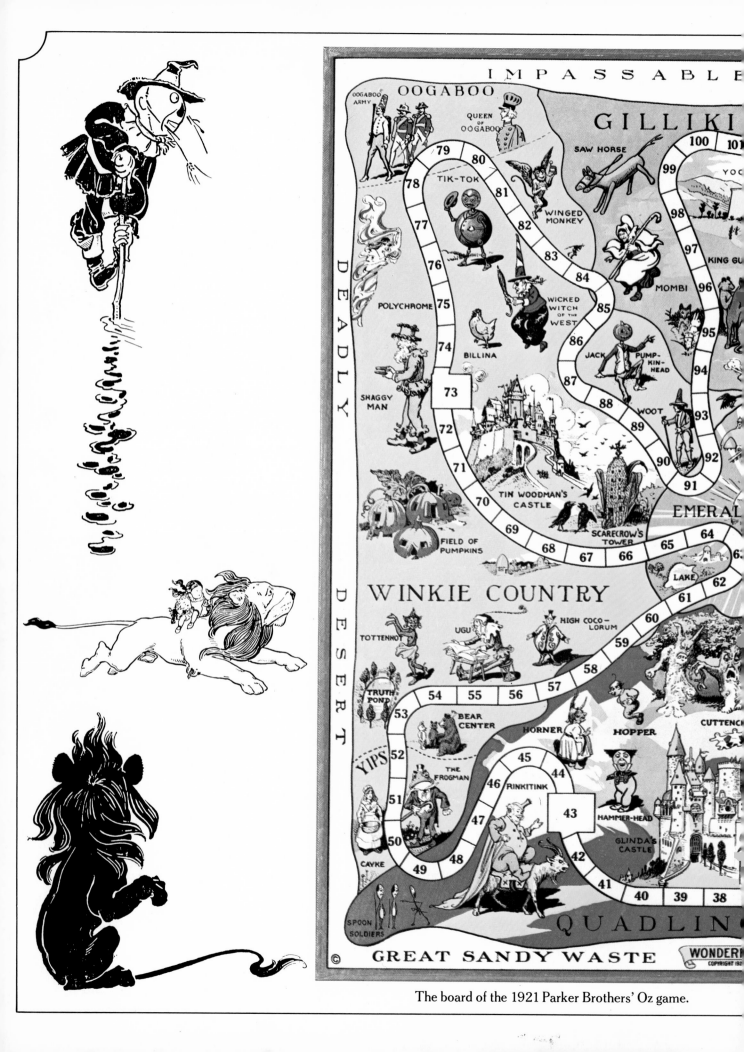

The board of the 1921 Parker Brothers' Oz game.

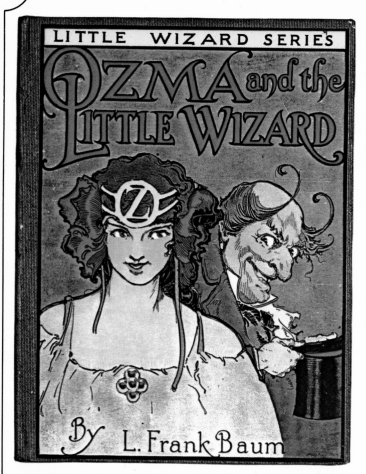

LITTLE WIZARD SERIES

OZMA and the LITTLE WIZARD

By L. Frank Baum

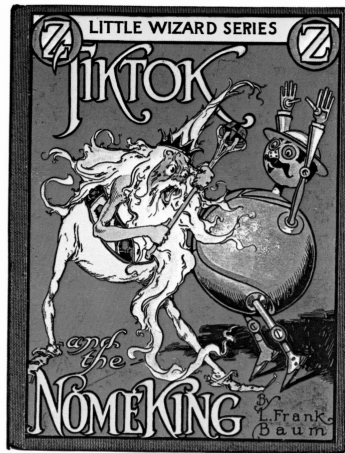

LITTLE WIZARD SERIES

TIKTOK and the NOME KING

By L. Frank Baum

JACK PUMPKINHEAD and the SAWHORSE

By L. Frank Baum

LITTLE WIZARD SERIES

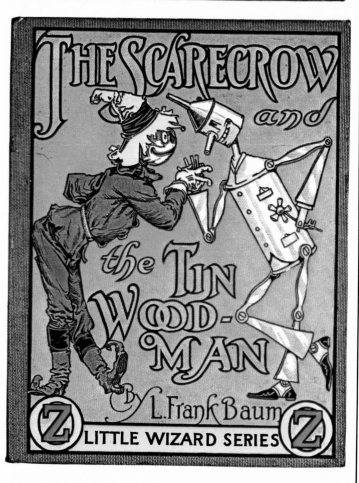

THE SCARECROW and the TIN WOOD-MAN

By L. Frank Baum

LITTLE WIZARD SERIES

The half title page in the original edition of *The Patchwork Girl of Oz* (1913).

Kabumpo in Oz

By
Ruth Plumly Thompson

Founded on and Continuing
The Famous Oz Stories
by L. FRANK BAUM
Pictures by John R. Neill

The new Oz book for 1922.

HANDY MANDY

IN OZ

Emerald City

Winkies

Quadlings

by Ruth Plumly Thompson

FOUNDED ON AND CONTINUING THE FAMOUS·OZ·STORIES

Gillikins

by L. Frank Baum

Munchkins

Illustrated by John R. Neill

The Oz book for 1937.

THE SCALAWAGONS OF OZ

by John R. Neill

founded on and continuing the famous Oz stories

by L. Frank Baum

The Oz book for 1941.

One of the many newspaper obituaries of L. Frank Baum.

The Flatheads, from *Glinda of Oz.*

THE POST-INTELLIGENCER.

SEATTLE, SUNDAY, JULY 13, 1919.

Frank Baum, Who Found American Fairies Like Those in "Alice in Wonderland" Made Himself Immortal to American Children

Discovered the Enchanted "Land of Oz" and Its Tin Woodman, Wogglebug, Glass Cat, Tik-Tok, and Other Whimsical Brain Creatures Which, Though Their Creator Has Died, Will Live On and On in the Hearts of Kiddies Who Read the Books He Put Them In.

By Marguerite Moers Marshall

THE maker of fairies is dead. His other name is L. Frank Baum, who set a country laughing seventeen years ago with "The Wizard of Oz," and followed it up with a dozen charming fairy books of the mythical kingdom to which, by means of a Kansas cyclone, he had transported little Dorothy Gale and her pet calf. In the land of Oz she met the Glass Cat, the Crooked Magician, the Giant Porcupine, the Tin Woodman, the Yellow Hen, the Wogglebug and many other enchanting beings.

"The American Lewis Carroll" Baum has been called. He was born in the state of New York, and although he was living in Los Angeles at the time of his death and made his first success in Chicago, it was for the children of New York that he wished to make true his dearest dream—a children's theater. He did succeed in giving a charming group of "fairylogues" at the Hudson theater, and he had thousands of friends in this city.

"I am almost sure," he writes modestly in the preface to "Tik-Tok of Oz," "that I have as many friends among the children of America as any story writer alive; and this, of course, makes me very proud and happy." And in "The Tin Woodman of Oz," which appeared only last year, he says: "My books are intended for all those whose hearts are young, no matter what their ages may be." In these two sentences there is a picture of the happy relations existing between his public and the "Royal Historian of Oz."

The Oz books, all of which are published by the Reilly & Britton Company, of Chicago, include, in their order: "The Land of Oz," "Ozma of Oz," "Dorothy and the Wizard in Oz," "The Road to Oz," "The Emerald City of Oz," "The Patchwork Girl of Oz," "Tik-Tok of Oz," "The Lost Princess of Oz" and "The Tin Woodman of Oz."

"Ozma of Oz" is the tale of how Dorothy Gale and her wonderful friends, after many adventures, free the beautiful Queen of Ev, and her ten children, who had been sold by their cruel father to the king of the Nomes and had been turned by him into ornaments for his palace.

The king promises Dorothy to let them go if she and those with her detect them among all the other bric-a-brac in his palace—a task well nigh impossible. After elven vain guesses each member of Dorothy's party is turned into an ornament. Dorothy herself escapes this fate, since she guesses correctly that a purple china kitten is one of the enchanted children.

Finally, Billina, the yellow hen, saves the day. Hiding under the throne of the king of the Nomes, she has heard him talking about his enchantment methods, and all her guesses are correct. Then she also brings to life the Tin Woodman and his army, the Scarecrow, the little Queen Ozma of Oz and the others of Dorothy's party, who have been enchanted by the wicked king.

In his rage he tries to hold them prisoners, but once more Billina comes to the rescue. At her suggestion the Scarecrow pulls from his pocket two of Billina's own eggs—rank poison to Nomes—and hurls them into the face of the king. While he is blinded and terrified Dorothy takes off his magic belt, and his power is at an end.

The book is full of charming whimsicalities. One of its most amusing characters is the Hungry Tiger, who wears a pink ribbon on his tail and is always hungry. When Dorothy asks him why he doesn't eat he says it's no use as he always gets hungry again. And he has an appetite for all sorts of living creatures, from a chipmunk to fat babies.

"Fat babies!" he muses. "Don't they sound delicious? But I've never eaten any, because my conscience tells me it is wrong. If I had no conscience I would probably eat the babies and then get hungry again, which would mean that I had sacrificed the poor babies for nothing. No; hungry I was born, and hungry I shall die. But I'll not have any cruel deeds on my conscience to be sorry for. I am a good beast, perhaps, but a disgracefully bad tiger."

Some of the old people, but an entirley new set of thrilling adventures, are in "The Tin Woodman of Oz." Instead of Dorothy, the human child—or as the Tin Woodman calls him, "the meat person"—who goes adventuring is a little boy, Woot the Wanderer. With the Tin Woodman and our old friend, the Scarecrow, he sets out to find and rescue the Woodman's old sweetheart, Nimmee-Amee, who has been made a slave to a wicked witch.

The first land through which they pass is Loonville, inhabited by rubber balloon folk, who every now and then explode and must have their punctures mended and be blown up once more. Then they visit Mrs. Yoop, the wicked giantess of Yoop castle. She is a regular Circe for transforming her victims, by Yookoohoo magic, into animals. Her canary was once the lovely Polychrome, daughter of the Rainbow. In no time Woot the Wanderer has been made a little green monkey, the Scarecrow has become a bear and the Tin Man a tin owl. They escape by stealing her magic apron.

In the wood they first meet with a jaguar who wants to eat them, but who is appeased by a magic breakfast of scrambled eggs and toast. Little Woot, however, in attempting to escape the beast by means of the magic apron which he still wears, sinks into the ground and wakes up a crowd of indignant dragons.

Luckily, when they are just on the verge of catching him, he remembers the apron and pops up through the earth as speedily as he popped down. The three companions travel on, encountering Tommy Kwikstep, an impossible little boy, who loved to run errands and therefore was given twenty legs by a witch; also a farm girl, Jinjur, with a quick temper and fields of cream puffs, chocolate caramels and macaroons?

Finally, Princess Ozma of Oz and Dorothy find the poor creatures and restore them to their original shapes. After other interesting but less perilous chapters in their history they reach the home of Nimmee-Amee, which is surrounded by a wall of solid air six feet thick and a mile high. The pilgrims enter it through a rabbit burrough, after Polychrome has magically made them tiny, but they find Nimmee-Amee happily married, and not too glad to see them. With the conclusion of a violent shower Polychrome hurries back to her rainbow home, and the others go their several ways after being entertained at the court of Oz.

"Do you believe in fairies?" Peter Pan used to ask.

The maker of fairies is dead. But he would be the first to tell his young and old child friends that fairies never die.

TIKTOK THE MACHINE MAN

KALIKO

THE SHAGGY MAN

DOROTHY AND BUTTON-BRIGHT

TOMMY KWIKSTEP THE ——-LEGGED MAN

THE SCARECROW OF OZ AND THE WOODEN HORSE

THE GNOME KING

THE TIN WOODMAN AND THE TIN SOLDIER

JACK PUMPKIN-HEAD

THE WHEELER

of the oldest mythic traditions. And the Lonesome Duck, who provides Trot and Cap'n Bill with magic toadstools to sit on, anticipates the modern preoccupation with alienation: it can bear the company of no other creature.

Glinda of Oz, Baum's final Oz book, begins with Ozma's discovery in Glinda's Great Book of Records that the Skeezers have declared war on the Flatheads. Since both peoples are in Oz, Ozma decides that it is her duty to bring about peace—a duty that she seems not to have felt strongly in previous books. She and Dorothy journey north and are imprisoned by the Skeezers. It takes Glinda herself to save them.

Glinda is the most tightly plotted of all of Baum's books. It is also as somber as *The Magic of Oz*. Its villains are proud, cruel and vindictive, without any of the comic touches that make us laugh at the Nome King. Magic is more mechanistic than it is in any other Oz book: the most important magic is no longer a simple device, but a complex machine, and the machine is more important than the person who makes it function. Even in a fairyland, technology, like war, can dehumanize.

Baum survived his operation, but it so strained his already weak heart that he spent his last year bedridden. He died at his home in Hollywood, California, on May 6, 1919, nine days before his sixty-third birthday. His last two Oz books were published posthumously. News of his death was telegraphed around the world, and newspapers of every size and type, from the *New York Times* to small country weeklies, eulogized America's greatest writer of fairy tales and praised his creation. The Land of Oz was a real place to millions of children and adults, and to many, Baum had seemed a personal friend. Now Baum was dead; Oz, of course, lives on.

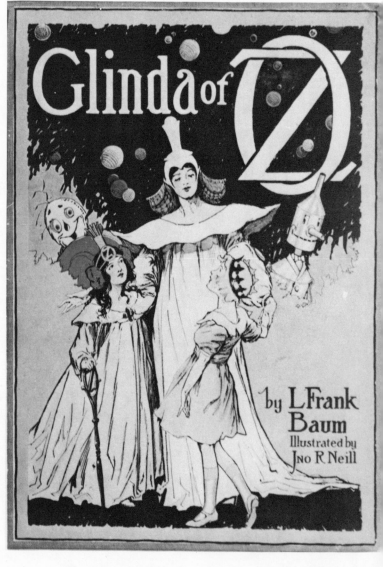

Later Explorers of Oz

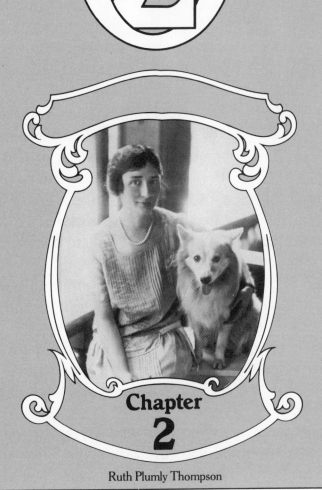

Chapter
2

Ruth Plumly Thompson

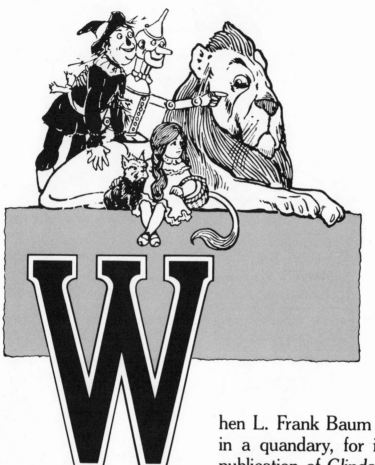

When L. Frank Baum died his publishers were in a quandary, for it seemed that after the publication of *Glinda of Oz,* America's most important and most lucrative series of fairy tales would come to an end. This would also create a problem for Baum's heirs, for the continued sales of the earlier titles depended on the publicity surrounding each year's new book. Reilly & Lee made a radical decision: they would find another author to continue the Oz books.

William F. Lee, vice-president of the company, was in charge of the search. Lee, who lived in Philadelphia, was impressed by the imaginative powers of Ruth Plumly Thompson, a twenty-nine-year-old Philadelphian who had been writing the weekly children's page for the Philadelphia *Public Ledger* since 1914. She had also had stories published in *St. Nicholas* magazine; and she had published one book of children's fantasy and sold another.

Miss Thompson, who had read and loved the Oz books since she was a child, was delighted with the proposal. Since she was the main support of her widowed mother and invalid sister, she also welcomed the virtual guarantee of a published book a year. The contracts were signed in 1920 with Miss Thompson and with Mrs. Baum, who was to receive a

royalty on each Thompson Oz book. The agreements provided that Miss Thompson's first Oz title would be published under Baum's name so that there would be a transition between the two authors. Later Oz books prominently featured the phrase, "Founded on and Continuing the Famous Oz Stories by L. Frank Baum." Miss Thompson's first contribution was *The Royal Book of Oz*, "by L. Frank Baum, Enlarged and Edited by Ruth Plumly Thompson." Actually it was entirely the work of Miss Thompson. Despite Baum's statement that he left material for the 1921 book, Miss Thompson used no Baum notes for *The Royal Book*.

The Kabumpo poster.

When Miss Thompson retired as Roya
Historian of Oz in 1939, she had writter
nineteen Oz books, five more than Baum

Ruth Plumly Thompson's Oz is buil
on Baum's, but she was not a slavish imita
tor. Her fairyland is filled with countries tha
seem like tiny German principalities, with
such delightful names as Kimbaloo, Baffle
burg, Regalia, Menankypoo, and best of all
Pumperdink, home of Kabumpo, the Elegan
Elephant of Oz. Miss Thompson's Oz is
nothing if not heterogeneous, for in or under
it we also find Mudge, a desert shiekdom
Moojer Mountain, with its elevator man
Blankenburg, an underground city with in
visible people; Down Town, with its King
Dad; the lovely lost lake of Orizon; the ori
ental Silver Islands; and, regrettably, Diksy
land. The list could be continued almost
indefinitely.

Miss Thompson was at her best with
an amazing variety of strange characters
Pigasus, a poetical flying pig; Reachard,
whose arm will stretch to reach anything; Si
Hokus of Pokes, an Arthurian knight; Cap
tain Salt of the good ship *Crescent Moon*—
again the list is endless. The most fondly
remembered, by children and adults alike,
of all her characters is Jinnicky, the Red Jinn
and Wizard of Ev. Jinnicky's torso is actually
encased in a giant red ginger jar, somewhat
like a turtle shell, and he uses the lid of the
jar for a hat. The Red Jinn is spoiled, petu-
lant, childish and warm-hearted.

Ruth Plumly Thompson had as fertile
an imagination as Baum, but she did not

THE REILLY & LEE CO.

A letter from John R. Neill, the artist,
About the 1922 Oz Book

593 Riverside Drive
New York City

Jan 12 22

Dear F. K. Reilly :–
Am sending today the last lot
of drawings, completing the illustrations for "Kabumpo in Oz"
Incidentally I would like to tell
you how much I enjoyed reading the
mss. and making the pictures.
After illustrating about seventeen Oz books I think it worth while
to let you know this with my congrat-
ulations on having secured an author
of such superior qualifications
to continue the work of supplying
the "Oz books"
Every feature of the child
appeal is handled with the greatest
skill. The whimsical the humor the
interest and the Zip of the book
makes me think it one of the very best
Oz books so far.
Sincerely .
Jno R Neill

"Kabumpo in Oz" will be Published May 1.

All of the OZ books (Kabumpo is No. 15) sell every day in the year—from Jan. 1 to Dec. 31.

Plan to display the new OZ book on May 1 and you'll have a big OZ sale for eight straight months!

We Shall Have a Wonderful "Kabumpo" Poster!

In their 1922 catalogue, Reilly & Lee gave a full page to the first Oz book published under Ruth Plumly Thompson's name.

take her work so seriously. The faults found occasionally in Baum's books occur frequently in Miss Thompson's. All her books are primarily tours of Oz or the lands and oceans around it. She herself said that she had no real idea where a book would go once she started writing it. But despite many stops along the way, all quests in her books are realized. Miss Thompson's stories frequently show her respect for Baum. Sometimes she displays great ingenuity in tying up some of the loose ends in the books of the first Royal Historian. For example, in *The Lost King of Oz* (1925), Ozma's long-missing father, King Pastoria, who was mentioned only briefly by Baum, is found again, with a carefully constructed account of his exile; *Ojo of Oz* (1933) provides Ojo with parents; and *The Royal Book of Oz* explains why the Scarecrow, unlike all others of his kind, is alive.

Jinnicky, the Red Jinn of Ev.

The HUNGRY TIGER of OZ

By Ruth Plumly Thompson

Founded on and Continuing

The Famous Oz Stories By L. Frank Baum

Illustrated by Jno. R. Neill

THE GNOME KING OF OZ

By Ruth Plumly Thompson

Founded on and Continuing

The Famous Oz Stories By L. Frank Baum

Illustrated by Jno. R. Neill

The GIANT HORSE of OZ

By Ruth Plumly Thompson

FOUNDED ON AND CONTINUING

The Famous Oz Stories By L. Frank Baum

ILLUSTRATED BY Jno. R. Neill

JACK PUMPKINHEAD OF OZ

By Ruth Plumly Thompson

FOUNDED ON, AND CONTINUING

The Famous Oz Stories by L. Frank Baum

ILLUSTRATED by JNO R NEILL

SPEEDY IN OZ

RUTH PLUMLY THOMPSON

FOUNDED ON AND CONTINUING THE FAMOUS OZ STORIES BY L FRANK BAUM

ILLUSTRATED BY JNO R NEILL

THE WISHING HORSE OF OZ

by Ruth Plumly Thompson founded on and continuing the famous Oz stories by L. Frank Baum Illustrated by Jno R Neill

CAPTAIN SALT IN OZ

By Ruth Plumly Thompson

FOUNDED ON AND CONTINUING THE FAMOUS-OZ-STORIES by L. Frank Baum

Illustrated by John R Neill

THE SILVER PRINCESS IN OZ

By Ruth Plumly Thompson

FOUNDED ON AND CONTINUING The Famous Oz Stories By L. Frank Baum

ILLUSTRATED BY JNO. R. NEILL

Ruth Plumly Thompson around 1927 with actors in her play, *A Day in Oz*, which was performed in department stores to promote the books. The girl at the upper left is her sister, Janet.

See the Tin Woodman and the Scarecrow

from the

Land of Oz

are arranging a delightful Hallowe'en Program

at Bullock's.

The Oz Playlet

will be given as a special courtesy to Olde Witch and her troupe of Ghosts, Witches, Jack' o Lanterns, etc.

Dorothy and the Patchwork Girl are making elaborate plans for the event and urge you, most cordially, to be present.

The day, the hour and all details regarding the program will be found on the other side of this sheet.

Didja ever hear of Oz?

Now didja ever, ever, ever?
It's sixty-seven thousand leagues
Beyond the land of Never.

Surrounded by a deadly desert,
But when once you're there
It's better than a circus
Or a zoo or anywhere.
'Cause animals in Oz can talk,
And so of course, they do.
No roars or prowls, meows or howls,
They just say "How are you!"

And all the days in Oz are fine,
And most of them are sunny,
And all the fairy folk in Oz
Are queer and dear and funny.

But since you can't all go to Oz,
We've brought a very few
Of the dear delightful Oz-folks here,
To talk and sing to you.

A department-store program for *A Day in Oz*, here called simply *The Oz Playlet*. The program cover is shown on the opposite page.

Bullock's
Boys' and Girls' Store
Hallowe'en Program
Bullock's English Floor
Saturday Morning, October 31, 1925

Tickets of admission both for Children and Adults may be procured in the Boys' and Girls' Store at the Exchange Desk, Bullock's Fifth Floor, at any time previous to Saturday, October thirty-one.

Three separate programs will be given
9:30 A. M.
10:30 A. M.
11:30 A. M.

Tickets for adults will be collected at the entrance, but children are requested to retain theirs until the close of the Program when they will be exchanged for a souvenir.

Bullock's

There are dangers aplenty in Ruth Plumly Thompson's books, but none needs to be taken too seriously. The most important threats are from monarchs who try to conquer Oz. Miss Thompson uniformly depicts them as spoiled children. The former monarch of the Gnomes (Miss Thompson corrected Baum's spelling) makes the attempt in four more books. He is currently a cactus in the royal conservatory, having

The Oz Playlet

A Hallowe'en Program for Boys and Girls

Courtesy of

Bullock's Book Shop
Street Floor, Hill St. Building
Los Angeles

November 7, 1925   1595

The window display for "A Day In Oz" is part of an elaborate Children's Book Week feature prepared by Reilly and Lee

"A Day In Oz"

The Tin Woodman and the Cowardly Lion Are Appearing in Many Communities This Fall to Help Celebrate Book Week

AN ingenious advertising scheme in line with Children's Book Week publicity is that of Reilly and Lee for pushing their Oz books, a scheme that has gained the booksellers' cooperation.

A playlet, "A Day in Oz" or "Scraps from Oz" which can be easily and simply staged and which plays about thirty to forty minutes has been written by Miss Ruth Plumly Thompson who has carried on the writing of the Oz books since the death of their creator, Lyman Frank Baum. The characters in the play are Scraps, the Patchwork Girl; Princess Ozma, the ruler of Oz; the Tin Woodman, Little Dorothy, the Scarecrow and the Cowardly Lion. All costumes, except that of Dorothy which is a simple gingham dress, made to fit boys and girls of 10 to 15 are furnished by Reilly and Lee. There are four songs for which music has been written by Norman Sherrerd, the well-known Philadelphia composer—"The Scarecrow's Song," "Tin Woodman's Song," "Song of the Wizard

of Oz" and "Song of the Cowardly Lion." Copies of the play and music are obtainable from the Oz publishers as well as souvenirs to be distributed at the end of the play.

To make the play a complete success, window and interior display material will also be furnished. A number of booksellers have made arrangements for the production of the playlet, linking up their window and table displays and benefiting by the publicity that the performance would get.

The Oz playlet at the Washington Book Fair of Woodward & Lothrop was a huge success. Miss Thompson was present and supervised the production of her play.

Meier & Frank Co., of Portland, Ore., on the day of their performance of the play sold about one hundred copies of the Oz books and in addition stimulated a great deal of interest for their Christmas business.

been given that shape after his last (but not necessarily final) failure.

The Thompson Oz books were heralded with a Neill cutout poster for *Kabumpo in Oz*, and the 1922 Reilly & Lee catalogue carried a letter from the illustrator praising the book. The 1920's were filled with plans for Oz promotions and gimmicks. One of the most successful was Miss Thompson's 1925 playlet, "A Day in Oz, or Scraps from Oz." The plot, about a party given by Dorothy, promoted each year's new Oz book. Reilly & Lee distributed the play to bookstores and department stores, which found schoolchildren to act in it. Costumes were provided by the publisher, along with printed sheet music by Norman Sherrerd. (Miss Thompson's songs and Sherrerd's music were written in 1924, as part of an unsuccessful attempt to convince recording firms—notably Victor Talking Machine Company—to record them for children.) During the 1920's Reilly & Lee also dis-

THE SCARECROW of OZ

Pastoria, Father of Princess Ozma No. 18

The Capitol of Ozma's Kingdom No. 5

The Scarecrow washed her out with water No. 18

A patchwork doll, brought to life No. 6

"The Tin Woodman" No. 11

A wise man with bran brains No. 8

"Glinda of Oz" No. 13

In Fairyland No. 1

Because he was afraid of Mombi No. 10

Dorothy Gale of Kansas No. 3

The Elegant Elephant of Pumperdink No. 15

The Little Wizard of Oz No. 12

ANSWERS QUESTIONS BY RADIO

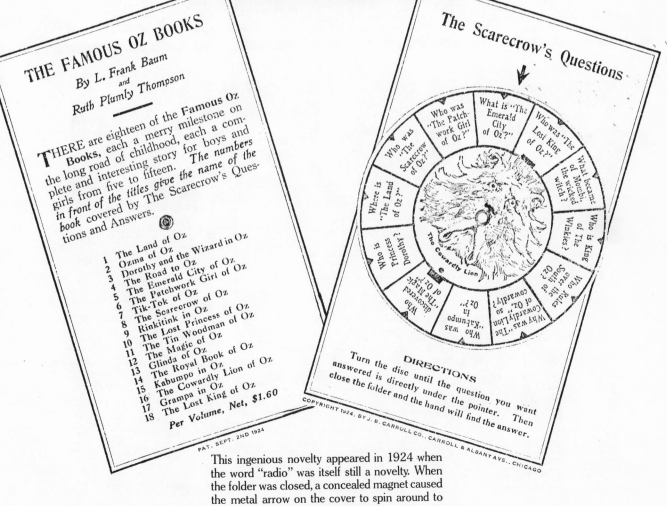

THE FAMOUS OZ BOOKS

By L. Frank Baum and Ruth Plumly Thompson

THERE are eighteen of the **Famous Oz Books**, each a merry milestone on the long road of childhood, each a complete and interesting story for boys and girls from five to fifteen. *The numbers in front of the titles give the name of the book covered by The Scarecrow's Questions and Answers.*

1 The Land of Oz
2 Ozma of Oz
3 Dorothy and the Wizard in Oz
4 The Road to Oz
5 The Emerald City of Oz
6 The Patchwork Girl of Oz
7 Tik-Tok of Oz
8 The Scarecrow of Oz
9 Rinkitink in Oz
10 The Lost Princess of Oz
11 The Tin Woodman of Oz
12 The Magic of Oz
13 Glinda of Oz
14 The Royal Book of Oz
15 Kabumpo in Oz
16 The Cowardly Lion of Oz
17 Grampa in Oz
18 The Lost King of Oz

Per Volume, Net, $1.60

PAT. SEPT. 2ND 1924

The Scarecrow's Questions

Who was "The Scarecrow of Oz?"

Who was "The Patchwork Girl of Oz?"

What is "The Emerald City of Oz?"

Who was "The Lost King of Oz?"

Where is "The Land of Oz?"

What became of Mombi the wicked witch?

Who is King over the Winkies?

Who is Princess Dorothy?

Who is King over the South of Oz?

Who discovered "The Magic of Oz?"

Why was "The Cowardly Lion so cowardly?"

Who was "The Cowardly Lion of Kabumpo in Oz?"

The Cowardly Lion

DIRECTIONS

Turn the disc until the question you want answered is directly under the pointer. Then close the folder and the hand will find the answer.

This ingenious novelty appeared in 1924 when the word "radio" was itself still a novelty. When the folder was closed, a concealed magnet caused the metal arrow on the cover to spin around to the correct answer.

READ THIS FAN MAIL

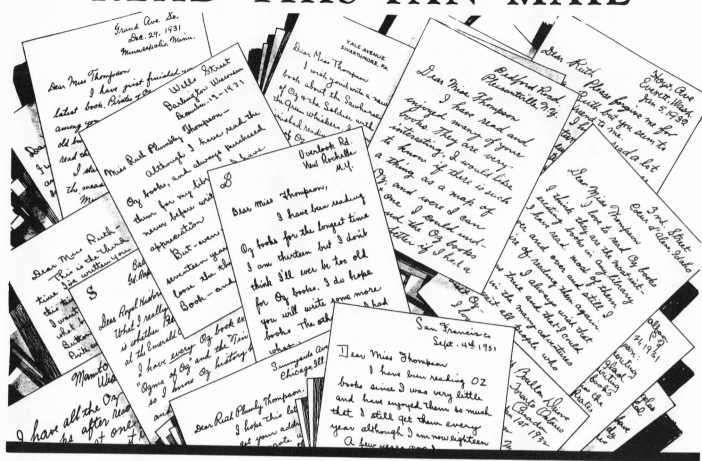

THE WONDERLAND OF OZ   No. 1.
Based on the stories by L. Frank Baum

In the country of the Gillikens, which is in the north of the land of Oz, lived a youth called Tip. There was more to his name than that, for old Mombi, with whom he lived, often declared that his whole name was Tippetarius but no one could be expected to say all that when just Tip would do. Old Mombi, it must be confessed, was not very kind to Tip. She made him perform many hard tasks and often beat him.

Tip and old Mombi lived in one of the dome-shaped farm houses which are peculiar to the land of Oz. One or two neighbors lived nearby, but as there were no children for many miles, Tip had no playmates. For this reason, Tip did not find life so hard as you might suppose. Like most young boys, he managed to steal time from his tasks to go walking in the woods, to chase rabbits, and to gather hickory nuts in the fall.

One of Tip's most important duties was to milk the four-horned cow which was Mombi's especial pride. Early in the morning before sunrise, he would go out to the stable to brush and milk the cow. After that he would carry wood for the fire, fetch the water, and finally, after breakfast wash the dishes. Then, old Mombi would set him to work in the fields. But Tip would often slip away from his task to play. Consequently he grew to be a strong and healthy boy.

But despite the fact that life was not as unpleasant for Tip as it might have been, the boy frankly hated old Mombi. His dislike for her was shared by others, too, for the old woman did not enjoy the best of reputations. Her neighbors, the Gilliken people, had reason to suspect her of indulging in magic arts, and therefore both feared her and hesitated to associate with her.

Copyrighted 1932, The Reilly & Lee Co.

THE WONDERLAND OF OZ   No. 2.
Based on the stories by L. Frank Baum

But while old Mombi practiced magic arts, she was not exactly a witch. The good witch who ruled over that part of Oz had forbidden any other witch to exist in her dominions. So Tip's guardian, much as she might aspire to working magic, realized that it was unlawful to be more than a sorceress, or at most, a wizardess. However, she practiced her magic art as much as she dared, and often stayed up all night muttering incantations over her strange potions.

One morning, before sending Tip out to work in the fields, old Mombi called him. She was going, she said, to a nearby village for groceries, and would be gone for two days. She was really going to visit a powerful wizard. Although Tip knew this, he was glad to see the old woman go, and immediately began making plans for play while she was gone.

In old Mombi's cornfield there also grew many pumpkins. When Mombi was at home Tip went every day to hoe the weeds from these fields. But this day he went for a different purpose. Picking the largest and ripest pumpkin, he started to carve a face into it, just the way American children do at Hallowe'en when they make a Jack o' Lantern. With this he planned to frighten old Mombi on her return.

Not having any playmates, Tip did not know that boys often dig out the inside of a "pumpkin head," and in the space thus made put a lighted candle to make the face more startling. But he conceived an idea of his own that promised to be quite as effective. He decided to manufacture the form of a man who would wear the pumpkin head. So he went to the woods and soon had the man's body completed. "When old Mombi sees this," he said, "she'll squeal with fright."

Copyrighted 1932, The Reilly & Lee Co.

A page from a promotional leaflet for the 1932-33 comic strip.

tributed another promotional play: "School-days in the Land of Oz," by Eleanor T. MacMillan.

A more interesting literary effort is "The Enchanted Tree of Oz," an unfinished Thompson short story written for *Topsy Turvy Time*, a children's radio show broadcast daily over WMAQ in Chicago. With the encouragement of Reilly & Lee, stories from the Oz books were read on the program during 1926 and 1927, and the Thompson story was part of a contest to which children submitted endings. A tantalizing tale it is

---

The front page of the 1928 edition of the *Ozmapolitan*.

too, for it shows Dorothy and the Scarecrow disappearing into the magical Tree of Whutter Wee—and then the story stops.

The mid-1920's were banner years for Oz publicity. In 1925 Reilly & Lee manufactured a magnetic question-and-answer novelty called "The Scarecrow of OZ Answers Questions by Radio" and distributed black-and-white versions of the Oz maps first made in 1914 (see page 44) for a coloring contest. In 1926 and 1927 it used wooden cutout figures of the Scarecrow and the Patchwork Girl to promote the current Oz book, and in 1926 it published the first issue of the revived *Ozmapolitan* (later issues appeared in 1927 and 1928). The 1926 *Ozmapolitan* let children around the country know about the Ozmite Club, which had just been formed by the publishers and which was to last for two years. Ozmites received a metal pin, copies of *The Ozmapolitan*, the "Secrets" (which were so secret that no copy is known to survive), and "invitations to the Oz parties"—probably performances of "A Day in Oz" at local stores. With all these promotions, it is strange that Reilly & Lee rejected Miss Thompson's suggestion that the dedication to the 1925 Oz book, *The Lost King of Oz*, be a crossword puzzle. The publisher erroneously believed that the crossword-puzzle craze would soon die out and that using the device would date the book.

The Baum Oz books had been syndicated in newspapers with success throughout the 1920's, and in 1932 the publisher was encouraged to try another Oz comic. *The Wonderland of Oz* was distributed by C. C. Winningham, Inc., of Detroit. The artist was Walt Spouse, who based his conceptions entirely upon Neill's drawings. Ultimately, five books appeared in comic form: *The Land of Oz, Ozma of Oz, The Emerald City of Oz, The Patchwork Girl of Oz* and

here they come!

Your Old Friends in a **NEW** Cartoon Serial

The **Wonderland of Oz**

from the popular fairy tales of L. Frank Baum

★ C. C. WINNINGHAM *Inc. Advertising and Merchandising* ★

Tik-Tok of Oz. All newspapers carrying the strip were doubtless sent publicity articles, and the Philadelphia *Evening Bulletin* for May 3, 1932, carried an interview with Miss Thompson. But *The Wonderland of Oz* failed, probably because Spouse's adaptations are so faithful to the original that many of the four-frame installments have very little action.

After the death of F. K. Reilly in 1932, there were few Oz promotions. The Oz series was long established and very popular, and the publishers believed that publicity beyond the advertisements for each year's book was no longer necessary. Many years later Miss Thompson described her frustration in trying unsuccessfully to convince Reilly & Lee to issue new versions of the Oz maps with places from the later books.

In 1935 Reilly & Lee was faced with a surprising problem: the first direct challenge to its exclusive right to publish new Oz books. The challenge came from a man with a justifiable belief in his own rights in the matter: L. Frank Baum's eldest son, Frank Joslyn Baum, who had written the script for the 1925 *Wizard of Oz* movie, had sold the rights for the forthcoming Metro-Goldwyn-Mayer movie, and had manufactured Oz dolls in 1924 (see page 175). Frank J. Baum had hoped to continue the Oz series after his father's death, but Reilly & Lee reached its agreement with Mrs. Baum and Miss Thompson. Sometime in the 1920's Frank J. Baum wrote an Oz book which Reilly & Lee refused to consider, and in 1932 it was advertised as a non-Oz book by the publisher David Graham Fischer of Hollywood under the title *Rosine and the Laughing Dragon.* It never appeared as such, but in January 1935 the Whitman Publishing Company of Racine, Wisconsin, published a portion of the manuscript under the title *The Laughing Dragon of Oz* by "Frank Baum." The

The Ozmite Club Pin

S S S S S S S S S S S S S S s s s sh!!

Boys . . . . Girls
Have You Heard About
THE OZMITE CLUB

THE Ozmite Club is a fun Club. *There are no dues.*
Membership entitles you to the *Secrets*, the beautiful
Ozmite Club Pin, copies of the *Ozmapolitan*, the official
newspaper of Oz and invitations to the *Oz Parties.*

Who Can Belong??
ANY boy or girl who loves the Oz folk or wants to read about their strange and wonderful
adventures recorded in the Oz Books.

How To Join??
Fill in the following blank. Sign your name plainly (at home or down town in the store.)

Check
One
of
these
Squares

☐ I am an Ozmite (One who loves the Oz Books)
I have read the Oz Books checked (see list on
back) and I want to belong to the Ozmite
Club.

☐ I have not read any of the Oz Books yet, but
I am interested and want to be an Ozmite.

If there are no members of the club in my neighborhood, I will do all I can to get my friends to join so we can get
together and enjoy the Ozmite Club and its activities.

Where to Join
When you have filled in the blanks properly, hand this sheet to the
lady in the book department and she will give you the beautiful
Ozmite Pin and Ozmite Secrets.

My Name Is_____

My Age Is _____

My Next Birthday Is_____

My Address Is___

My Telephone_

My Parents Name

Laughing Dragon was one of Whitman's many "Big Little Books," each of which had

around four hundred pages but was only four and a half inches tall. It was profusely illustrated by Milt Youngren, somewhat in the style of George Herriman's *Krazy Kat* comic. It sold for ten cents. *The Laughing Dragon* tells the story of Rosine, an American girl, her monkey Jim and Cap'n Bob, a lighthouse keeper, as they adventure in Oz seeking to rescue Princess Cozytoes. (The Laughing Dragon itself is a comical beast with a huge head and a tiny body; it joins the other adventurers.) No Oz characters from any other book appear in *The Laughing Dragon of Oz.* Frank J. Baum and Whitman planned to bring out a sequel entitled *The Enchanted Princess of Oz*, but while that work was in proof, Reilly & Lee brought

The cover of *The Laughing Dragon of Oz.* (Courtesy Joslyn S. Baum)

suit. The controversy was settled when Whitman agreed to pay court costs and not to publish *The Enchanted Princess.*

Reilly & Lee dropped color plates from the Oz books in 1935. Around the same time Ruth Plumly Thompson's imaginative powers (for yearly Oz books, at least) began to flag. Like Baum, she wanted to write other fantasies, and in 1938 David McKay published her *King Kojo.* Tension with Reilly & Lee over the publication and promotion of *King Kojo,* combined with financial disagreements and Miss Thompson's feeling that nineteen Oz books were enough for any author, led her to decide that *Ozoplaning with the Wizard of Oz* (1939) would be her last contribution to the series. She continued to write, primarily for magazines, but she did not totally escape Oz. In the early 1960's she wrote her twentieth Oz book, *Yankee in Oz,* which was published by the International Wizard of Oz Club in 1972, with illustrations by Dick Martin. In 1975 and 1976 she rewrote an unpublished manuscript of the late 1940's and made it an Oz book, *The Enchanted Island of Oz,* which was published by the Oz Club in 1976.

When she became Royal Historian of Oz, Miss Thompson followed Baum's example of answering all letters from children.

She was also gracious to adult enthusiasts, although as her niece, Dorothy Maryott, has written, "she could never truly understand people going back over her books and poking into details and what she meant and whether there was symbolism in this or that. She wrote for fun, for the sheer love of words and gay adventure, to entertain and amuse, and when she had finished a book or story it was finished, and that was that." Miss Thompson could laugh at herself and at serious critics of Oz. Some years ago she mentioned to a friend that a recent critic had found Freudian overtones in the fact that Baum's heroes were almost all pre-pubescent girls. "All my heroes are boys," she remarked; "I wonder what they would make of that."

Ruth Plumly Thompson died on April 6, 1976, at the age of eighty-four. Her twenty-one Oz books, uneven as they are, constitute a genuine contribution to the series. Although critical recognition—the sort of thing that did not bother her at all—is just beginning, her enthusiasts have always been legion.

When Miss Thompson retired from Oz in 1939, Reilly & Lee chose John R. Neill to continue the series. The choice seemed ideal, for Neill had illustrated all the Oz books except the first, and he had a fine imagination. Occasionally, in fact, his pictorial conceptions of certain characters are better than the author's. Unfortunately, the three Neill Oz books are the poorest in the series. They are highly imaginative, but

the imagination is undisciplined; each book, in fact, has enough ideas to fill several. What is even worse for the Oz enthusiast, Neill's concept of Oz is quite different from either Baum's or Thompson's. Miss Thompson occasionally tried to be contemporary by mentioning rockets or movie stunt men, but until *Ozoplaning with the Wizard of Oz* (which is in part about extraterrestrial travel in airplanes invented by the Wizard), she kept modernity in balance. Both Baum and Thompson realized that Oz must be timeless; despite the presence of various Americans, it cannot seem too much of the real world. Neill, however, was very modern indeed. *The Wonder City of Oz* (1940) deals with, among many other things, the "Ozlection" between Jenny Jump and Ozma for ruler of Oz, while *The Scalawagons of Oz* (1941) concerns live automobiles manufactured by the Wizard. As if that weren't enough, *Lucky Bucky in Oz* (1942) has Oz extend far beyond the Deadly Desert and says that all the rivers have been rolled up to protect the Scarecrow and the Tin Woodman, who both have an understandable aversion to water. The Neill books exaggerate Oz to the point where even the houses of the Emerald City are alive and get into occasional battles, and where the predominant color of each country is carried over into the tones of the sky and the skin of the inhabitants.

Before Neill's death in 1943 he had completed the text of *A Runaway in Oz*, and Reilly & Lee had announced it as the

Boys and Girls—

This is a very important message from Bucky Jones in Oz.

When I was blown off my father's tugboat back in New York harbor, I was blown into some risky adventures that might have scared me to death. Davy and I were in some very tight places; but every time we were almost beaten, somebody let us know he was helping us. Remember when Number Nine stopped the Gnomes, for instance? Nothing makes you so brave as knowing that somebody is helping you.

Now your fathers and uncles and older brothers are fighting a war. The Nazis and Japs are harder to beat than the Gnomes. Our soldiers will fight better and be braver if they know that the people back home are helping them. Everybody can help them. You certainly can.

The best way you can let them know you are helping is by buying Victory Bonds and Stamps right now and every time you have any money. No matter how many you already have, you can help by buying more. When you buy Bonds or Stamps you will know, and the soldiers will know, that part of their blankets and clothes and guns and tanks and planes are yours, bought with your money to help win the War. Buy more Stamps today and every chance you get. As a boy who has been helped in tight spots, I know how much it can mean.

Yours for Victory,

Bucky of Oz

A 1942 wartime letter from the hero of *Lucky Bucky in Oz* which was printed on the back jacket flap of the first edition.

Jack Snow's letterhead, designed by Frank Kramer.

JACK SNOW

Royal Historian of Oz

1943 Oz book. But it was never published. Apparently sales of recent Oz books were disappointing (the Baum Oz books have always sold well), and Reilly & Lee felt justified in waiting until the end of the war to resume the series.

The next Royal Historian was Jack Snow, most of whose life was involved in some way or other with Baum and Oz. Snow was born in 1907 in Piqua, Ohio. He first wrote to Reilly & Lee suggesting that he be Oz author when he was twelve. In high school he became involved with radio broadcasting during its earliest days, and eventually, after World War II, he joined the staff of the National Broadcasting Company. During the 1930's and 1940's he put together the finest Baum collection of the time, including the first editions of almost all the Baum books. He also interviewed Baum's relatives and friends for a proposed but never published Baum biography.

Snow was greatly interested in the strange, frequently morbid fantasy that appeared in the famous pulp magazine *Weird Tales*, which published a number of his stories, and in 1947 they and others were brought together in his collection *Dark Music and Other Spectral Tales*. Reilly & Lee had published his first Oz book, *The Magical Mimics in Oz*, the previous year, with illustrations by Frank Kramer. His second contribution to the series, *The Shaggy Man of Oz*, appeared in 1949, also

with Kramer illustrations, and his magisterial reference work, *Who's Who in Oz*, was published in 1954.

Snow's Oz books are conscious attempts to return to the Oz created by L. Frank Baum. No characters invented by Thompson or Neill are mentioned. The books are well plotted, and Snow had none of Neill's writing problems. He is at his best with his villains. Unfortunately, he was not especially good at humor, and he tried to duplicate Baum's work so closely that he imitated entire conversations, and in *The Shaggy Man*, adapted the plot of Baum's *John Dough and the Cherub* and used many of the places in that book.

Several contemporary comments indicate that Snow and Reilly & Lee planned to publish a new Oz book each year, but sales did not justify returning to that pattern. During the late 1940's Snow began to experience increasing financial and psychological problems, and these too may have had something to do with the delay between books. About 1949 Snow sold most of his Baum collection, and eventually he lost his position with NBC. In 1951 Reilly & Lee turned to another writer for a new Oz book. But in 1954 the publisher issued Snow's *Who's Who in Oz*, with brief biographical sketches of over six hundred Oz characters from all thirty-nine books then published. Despite occasional inaccuracies, it is a masterly work. But it did not sell well, which is doubtless why Reilly & Lee did not encourage Snow to go on with a new Oz book,

Jack Snow around 1940.

Rachel R. Cosgrove

Lauren McGraw Wagner and Eloise Jarvis McGraw.

tentatively entitled *Over the Rainbow to Oz.* It is a pity that the book was never written, for Snow's plans called for a long account of the early history of Oz, something he could have handled very well. Snow died on July 13, 1956, a month before his forty-ninth birthday.

In 1950 Rachel R. Cosgrove, a young research biologist, sent Reilly & Lee the manuscript for an Oz book. The publisher was impressed by it, and it was published in 1951 as *The Hidden Valley of Oz,* with illustrations by "Dirk" (Dirk Gringhuis). *The Hidden Valley* is closer to vintage Ruth Plumly Thompson than to anything by Neill or Snow. It has strange countries and villages and a fine villain: a giant whose size depends upon muffins from a magic tree. One of the best new characters is a leopard whose spots change shapes according to his mood. One of the worst is a giant rat who speaks slang from the late 1940's and calls himself Percy the Personality Kid.

In the early 1950's Miss Cosgrove wrote a sequel, *The Wicked Witches of Oz* (originally *Percy in Oz*), but Reilly & Lee eventually decided that the series was top-heavy and that any addition to it was unlikely to succeed financially. The firm had been shrinking since the early 1940's and now de-

pended primarily on the sales of the Oz books and the popular verse of Edgar Guest. In 1959 the fifty-seven-year-old publishing house was purchased by Henry Regnery Company, and thereafter the Reilly & Lee imprint was used mainly on children's books.

Regnery purchased Reilly & Lee primarily to acquire the Oz series. All the Oz books were officially in print, although in fact several had been "out of stock" for a number of years. All thirty-nine books were again made available, and a flock of new Oz publications began to appear. In 1960 Reilly & Lee published *The Visitors from Oz*, a large picture book based on Baum's 1904–5 comic page. This was followed by Russell P. MacFall's excellent Baum biography, *To Please a Child* (1961) by a series of Oz abridgements (1961) and finally by a new Oz book.

Merry Go Round in Oz, the fortieth Oz book, was written by Eloise Jarvis McGraw, a distinguished writer for children, and her daughter, Lauren McGraw Wagner, an artist and librarian. In 1962, at the urging of her daughter, Mrs. McGraw had her agent check with Regnery on whether further additions to the Oz series were being considered. Regnery was interested in seeing whether the interest in new Oz books could be revived and accepted Mrs. McGraw's manuscript (the writing was done by Mrs. McGraw, with considerable assistance in plot and characters from her daughter). The book was published in 1963 under the Reilly & Lee imprint, with illustrations by Dick Martin.

Dick Martin's front cover for the autumn 1976
Baum Bugle, an issue that paid tribute to Ruth
Plumly Thompson. (Courtesy *The Baum Bugle*)

Merry Go Round is an excellent book. It features Robin Brown, a young Oregon boy, and a living merry-go-round horse. The dual plot (a search, somewhat surprisingly, for the Easter Bunny, and the quest for the magic circlets of the kingdom of Halidom) combines Miss Thompson's delight in strange peoples and places with Baum's more serious concern with theme.

Regnery publicized the book heavily and even revived *The Ozmapolitan* for the first time since 1928, but *Merry Go Round* did not sell well enough to justify an Oz revival. There are no plans for further Oz books, although Regnery has authorized the Oz Club to publish the two recent Ruth Plumly Thompson Oz books and *Oziana*, an annual of original stories about Oz. The fourteen Baum Oz books have lately been reissued in a handsome new format, but all later titles have been allowed to go out of print.

The
Iconography
of Oz

Chapter
3

W. W. Denslow (top) and John R. Neill (bottom)

The Oz books have almost always been fortunate in their illustrators. In the words of Bobbs-Merrill's promotion for its 1939 reissue of *The Wizard*, "W. W. Denslow was the perfect collaborator for L. Frank Baum. His pictures could no more be separated from the text than Gilbert's words could be taken from Sullivan's music." Even in 1900, when the book was first published, reviewers remarked that it would be difficult to decide whether the artist drew the pictures to illustrate the tale or the author wrote the story to describe the pictures. Denslow's drawings are as much a part of *The Wizard* as Tenniel's are of *Alice*, Shepard's of *Winnie the Pooh*, or Cruikshank's of *Oliver Twist*.

William Wallace Denslow, one of America's most innovative illustrators, was born in 1856 in Philadelphia, studied at the Cooper Institute and the National Academy of Design in New York, and during the 1880's and 1890's, was primarily a newspaper cartoonist who wandered from place to place—New York, Maine, Philadelphia, Chicago, Denver, San Francisco, and back to Chicago. In Chicago he developed his own distinctive style, partly under the influence of such Art Nouveau illustrators as Will Bradley. He became a major designer of posters and book jackets and an important influence on many younger illustrators, including, somewhat later, John R. Neill.

This color plate of Dorothy punishing the Cowardly Lion, from *The Wonderful Wizard of Oz*, is a good example of Denslow's mannered, decorative style.

Chapter VIII.
The Deadly
Poppy Field.

In this chapter title from *The Wonderful Wizard of Oz*, Denslow's ornamental treatment of the poppies and the absolute repose of Dorothy and Toto make the episode less disturbing to children.

Denslow's drawings of the Cowardly Lion are impressive. With an economy of line he helped readers sympathize with the lion by showing him wiping his eyes with his own tail or, on facing page, cowering in fear.

Denslow's somewhat rakish Guardian of the Gate of the Emerald City.

In the first edition of *The Wonderful Wizard of Oz* Denslow established for all time the appearance of the Scarecrow, the Tin Woodman and the Cowardly Lion, and he was marvelously successful in endowing them with the attributes described by the author. They are by turns funny, absurd, pathetic, courageous, dignified, even noble—and at all times endearing. He was equally successful with almost all the other characters: the Wizard, the Guardian of the Gates, the Green-Whiskered Soldier, Doro-

The Wicked Witch of the West, with her three hair bows, spats and umbrella, threatens Toto.

Whatever qualities the Scarecrow, the Tin Woodman and the Cowardly Lion have just received from the Wizard, in the picture at right, humility is not one of them.

In *Denslow's Scarecrow and the Tin-Man* comic page (1904–5) and pamphlet, above and on next page, those two characters and the Cowardly Lion show as great a propensity for getting into difficulties as they did in *The Wonderful Wizard of Oz*, although their adventures now are in America with railroad trains and automobiles rather than wicked witches.

thy's little dog, Toto. His Glinda has an Art Nouveau graciousness, and his villains are properly frightening. The Wicked Witch of the West is ugly, menacing and absurd, with her eye patch, spats, umbrella and three pigtails, each tied with a bow; his Winged Monkeys look dangerously mischievous. When Metro-Goldwyn-Mayer filmed *The Wizard* in 1939 it wisely, though somewhat freely, based its characters upon Denslow's concepts. (Visually, however, Judy Garland was a distinct improvement on Denslow's drawings of Dorothy; in 1900 reviewers had already pointed out one of Denslow's few flaws: he could not draw a childlike child.)

An end-sheet illustration from *Denslow's Scarecrow and the Tin-Man and Other Stories* (1904).

Evelyn Copelman's beautifully drawn illustrations for Bobbs-Merrill's 1944 edition of *The Wizard of Oz* are somber and brooding. (© 1944 by The Bobbs-Merrill Co., Inc.)

Over the years many other artists have taken on the task of illustrating *The Wizard*, and it is not surprising that the most successful have been those who stayed closest to the models supplied by Denslow. One of the best was Dale Ulrey, whose illustrations for Reilly & Lee's 1956 *Wizard* show nearly as much lively humor as Denslow's, and also a grace and élan that are entirely her own. (Her illustrations for Reilly & Lee's 1955 edition of *The Tin Woodman of Oz* reveal the same exuberance and careful draftsmanship.)

Although in 1939 Bobbs-Merrill said that Baum's text and Denslow's illustrations were inseparable, in 1949 it separated them

by publishing a new edition of *The Wizard* with illustrations by Evelyn Copelman. From 1944 until 1956, when *The Wizard of Oz* entered the public domain, there was no edition available with Denslow's drawings. Copelman's illustrations are not, despite the publisher's claim, adapted from Denslow's

Dale Ulrey's drawings for Reilly & Lee's 1956 edition of *The Wizard* are humorous and filled with action.

Saturday Evening. THE MINNEAPOLIS JOURNAL. January 14, 1905

Denslow's SCARECROW and TINMAN on the WATER.

Written and Illustrated by W. W. Denslow the Illustrator of 'The WIZARD of OZ" and 'The PEARL and the PUMPKIN".

An episode from *Denslow's Scarecrow and the Tin-Man* comic page. In the frame at the lower right, Denslow himself greets the Scarecrow.

Cover design and a text illustration by Wolny Alexandru for a 1965 Rumanian edition of *The Wizard* (Bucharest: Editura Tineretalui). Alexandru's flirtatious Tin Woodman is especially interesting.

pictures, and her concepts of the characters owe as much to the M-G-M movie as they do to Denslow. Her pictures are beautifully drawn, yet her brooding somber-shadowed concepts of Oz are strangely unsatisfying to many readers.

Outside of this country, a number of artists have presented versions of Oz and the Oz characters. Except for several British versions of the Bobbs-Merrill edition with the Denslow illustrations, *The Wizard* was not available outside of the United States until *Le Magicien d'Oz* appeared in France in 1932. Since then, however, Dorothy and her friends have been depicted by artists in Japan, Taiwan, Spain, Sweden, Russia, China, Brazil, Rumania, Poland, Turkey, Hungary, Italy, Israel. The drawings are sometimes strange, often beautiful, and at times disturbing. Foreign illustrators have not felt limited by Denslow's or Neill's concepts, and while it is difficult to alter the Scarecrow or the Cowardly Lion greatly, they have drawn the Tin Woodman as everything from a rake with flirting eyes and a waxed mustache to an expressionless nonentity made of flat pieces of metal. A recent German edition even shows him with flatirons for feet and a teakettle for a head! Oz itself ranges from a country of medieval castles and villages to a land of sugary sweetness, to a nightmare world of gorgeous colors and atavistic terrors beyond anything that Baum could have imagined. But Oz is stubbornly American, and even the efforts of such notable illustrators as H. M. Brock in England and Maraja in Italy

Romain Simon's black-and-white Toto, expressionless Tin Woodman, made from flat pieces of metal, and other characters from *Le Magicien d'Oz* (1964). (Courtesy Libraire Hachette)

Der Zauberer Oz (1975). (Courtesy Cecilie Dressler Verlag) was illustrated by Franz Haacken, who showed great originality, especially with the Tin Woodman.

Frank L. Baum

ČAROVNIK IZ OZA

For Yugoslavian readers, Oz is depicted as a medieval fairyland by Maksim Sedej in *Čarovnik iz Oza* (Ljubljani: Mladinska Knjiga, 1959).

Some of the loveliest and most frightening Oz illustrations are those by the distinguished Czech illustrator, Arnošt Karásek, in *Čaroděj ze Země Oz* (Prague: Státní Nakladatelstiví Dětské Knihy, 1962). (Illustrations © 1962 by Arnošt Karásek)

Illustration by Helen Fisher from Sheila Lane's and Marion Kemp's English "Take Part" adaptation of *The Wizard of Oz* (Penguin Books, 1971; current edition published by Ward Lock Educational, Ltd.).

Dorothy and company in *Ozu no Maho Tsukai,* published in Tokyo by Kodansha, circa 1951. (Courtesy Kodansha International Ltd.)

The front cover of the Spanish edition, by Freixas (1940). (Courtesy Editorial Molino)

The cover of the Taiwan edition, *Lu Yeh Sien Tsung* (Taipei: Tsao-hsiung Ch'u-pan-she, 1962).

The Wicked Witch of the West and the leader of the Winged Monkeys by Freixas in *El Mago de Oz.* (Courtesy Editorial Molino)

The cover by N. Radlov of the 1939 edition of *Volshebnik Izumrudnogo Goroda* (Moscow & Leningrad: Ts. K.V.L.S.M. Publishing House of Children's Literature). This book is attributed to the Russian author Alexandr Volkov. (Courtesy *The Baum Bugle*)

don't quite capture the essence of the fairyland. (Perhaps this isn't surprising; no American illustrator has ever successfully conveyed the feeling of the London of Sherlock Holmes, and the only really satisfactory illustrations for *Pinocchio* are those of the Italian artist Attilio Mussino.)

The strangest phenomenon in foreign Oz books is the series of original Russian Oz stories by Alexandr Melentyevich Volkov. In 1939 Volkov published an adaptation of *The Wizard* in Moscow under the title *The Wizard of the Emerald City (Volshebnik Izumrudnovo Goroda)* and credited himself as author, with a brief acknowledgment to Baum. In this Russian version Dorothy became Ellie, Oz lost its name and there were several added adventures, including one with a giant who wants to put the little girl through his meat grinder. The original illustrations by N. Radlov are sketchy, and the book was inexpensively produced. It was reprinted in 1941. In the 1950's Volkov revised the story, and in 1959 it was published in a handsome edition with beautiful full-color illustrations on nearly every page by L. Vladimirski. *Volshebnik* was so popular that Volkov began a series of original sequels: *Urfin Dzhus and his Wooden Soldiers (Urfin Dzhus i yevo Dyerevyannie Soldati,* 1963), *Seven Underground Kings (Syem Pozyemnich Koroly,* 1969), *The Fire God of the Maronnes (Ognyennei Bog Marranov,* 1972), *The Yellow Fog (Zholti Tuman,* 1974), and *The Secret of the Deserted Castle (Taina Zabrosynnovo Zamka,* 1976).

Some of L. Vladimirski's fine illustrations for the 1959 edition of
Volshebnik Izumrudnogo Goroda (Moscow: Sovyetskiya Rossya).

A Hungarian view of the Emerald City: the front cover of *Oz, a Nagy Varázsló* (Budapest: Móra Könyvkiadó, 1966). (© 1966 by The Bobbs-Merrill Co., Inc.)

Maraja's illustrations for the Italian *Il Mago di Oz* (1957), which have also appeared in French and English editions, are lovely and wistful if not especially Oz-like. (Courtesy Fratelli Fabbri Editori)

Dorothy views the Emerald City: the cover by Mrs. Bena Gewirtz for *Hukosem Meieretz Utz* (1947). (Courtesy Izreel Publishing House)

All, with the possible exception of the last, which we haven't seen, are illustrated by Vladimirski and deal with various attempts to overthrow the rule of the Scarecrow. One or more American children appear in each book, as do the Iron Woodchopper and the Courageous Lion.

(Courtesy Fratelli Fabbri Editori)

The famous British illustrator H.M. Brock illustrated Hutchinson's 1947 edition of *The Wizard of Oz*. Although his pictures are bright and attractive, they fail to capture the personalities of Baum's characters.

(Courtesy Fratelli Fabbri Editori)

At almost exactly the same time that *Denslow's Scarecrow and the Tin-Man* comic strip was running in Sunday newspapers, other newspapers were carrying Baum's *Queer Visitors from the Marvelous Land of Oz*, illustrated by Walt McDougall. Though crudely drawn in the approved comic-page style of the period, McDougall's Oz characters are not without charm. McDougall's Dorothy is closer to the character in the musical comedy than the Dorothy in the book.

Two other early American Oz illustrators deserve brief mention before we come to Denslow's great successor, John R. Neill. Walt McDougall, the illustrator of Baum's 1904–5 comic page, *Queer Visitors from the Marvelous Land of Oz*, based his depictions on Neill's, but his Scarecrow is wobblier; his Jack Pumpkinhead is shorter and less appealing; his Woggle-Bug is more like an insect; and his Nick Chopper looks as if he were made of cast iron rather than tin. His illustrations are, however, filled with comic touches, one of the best of which is giving the Woggle-Bug a derby hat. Ike Morgan, who illustrated Baum's *Woggle-Bug Book* (1905), was another cartoonist who excelled in comedy, but since the only Oz character in *The Woggle-Bug Book* is the insect himself, Morgan added little to the depiction of Oz. His Woggle-Bug is based upon McDougall's.

Today Denslow is firmly established as the definitive illustrator of *The Wizard of Oz,* but the title, "Imperial Illustrator of Oz," belongs to John R. Neill, who illustrated

Tip Manufactures a Pumpkinhead

Neill's heading for the first chapter of *The Marvelous Land of Oz* shows his Ozian dwellings, each domed with chimneys on two sides and windows that make it appear a face.

John R. Neill's earliest versions of the Oz characters, from the second Oz book, *The Marvelous Land of Oz* (1904).

Neill's Dorothy was a more attractive little girl than Denslow's, as this pictorial comment in *The Road to Oz* (1909) suggests. Toto's contempt for the earlier Denslow version of himself seems a little unkind.

thirty-five Oz books (including the three that he wrote himself) and created the country pictorially.

John Rea Neill was twenty-six years old when he illustrated *The Marvelous Land of Oz.* When he died in September 1943, shortly before his sixty-seventh birthday, he was at work on his final Oz book.

Although Reilly & Britton/Lee had him illustrating one Oz project or another during most of his life, Neill managed to squeeze in many other activities. In fact, he generally seems to have considered Oz merely an annual chore, albeit a pleasant and lucrative one. Born in Philadelphia, he studied at the Pennsylvania Academy of Fine Arts and began his career in Philadelphia newspapers. A very fast worker, he was soon illustrating comic pages and magazine stories and books for as many as ten different publishers. His drawings appeared in most of the major magazines—*Saturday Evening Post, Ladies' Home Journal, Boys' Life, Pictorial Review, Delineator, Century*—as well as in many of the lesser ones, and in the 1920's and 1930's he added pulp magazines to his list, including *Argosy*, the most popular of them all.

Neill was not only a prolific illustrator, he was also—when he wanted to be—a very good one. His style, though more derivative than Denslow's, added new dimensions to Oz. He could be bold and posterlike

This color plate for *Rinkitink in Oz* (1916) is full of hidden faces.

where that quality was appropriate, or lyrical and dreamlike. His illustrations capture perfectly the feel of the scenes, from the eerie, underground caverns of the Nome King to lacy, ethereal castles in the sky. The cluttered, claustrophobic witches' laboratories, the jeweled magnificence of the Emerald City, the whimsical décor of the Scarecrow's corn-ear-shaped tower—Neill conveyed all these as Denslow never could have. The typical Ozian dwelling—a round domed structure with twin chimneys—was Neill's own invention.

Typical of Neill's later work is this double-page drawing from *The Wonder City of Oz* (1940). Most of the houses are the typical Neill Ozian dwelling, but two have cups and saucers on their roofs.

MOMBI AT HER MAGICAL INCANTATIONS.

Neill was able to create perfectly the power of witchcraft,
as in this illustration from *The Marvelous Land of Oz*.

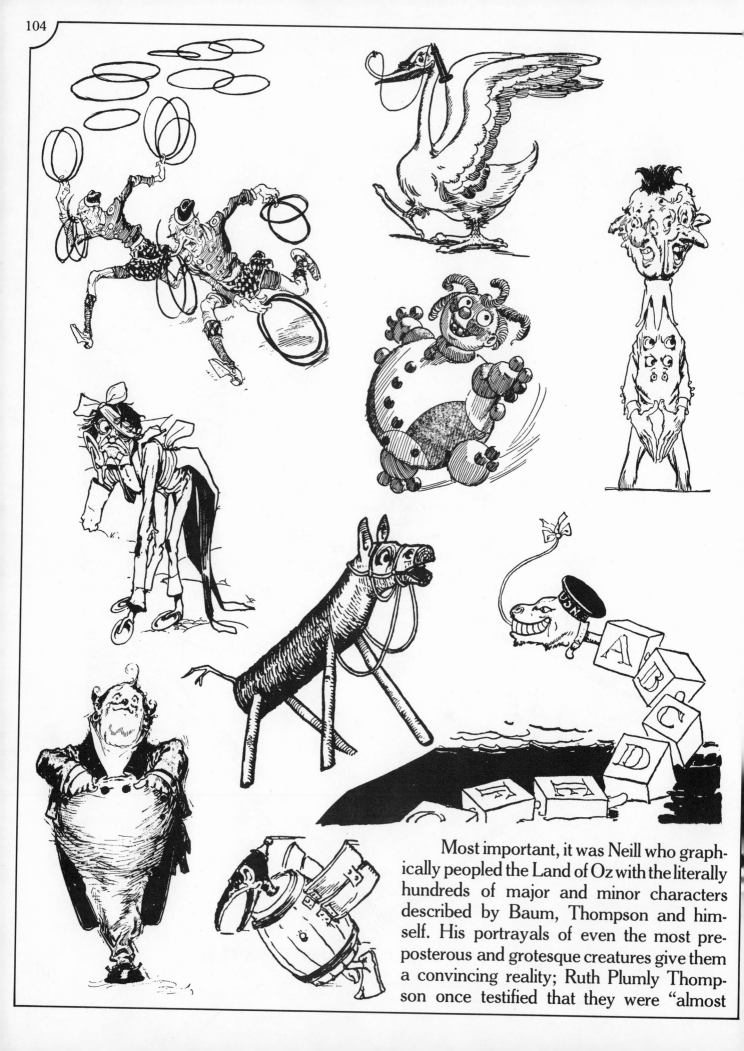

Most important, it was Neill who graphically peopled the Land of Oz with the literally hundreds of major and minor characters described by Baum, Thompson and himself. His portrayals of even the most preposterous and grotesque creatures give them a convincing reality; Ruth Plumly Thompson once testified that they were "almost

A gallery of grotesques: during four decades Neill depicted more than 400 of the curious denizens of Oz and managed to give each one a distinctive personality.

exactly as L. Frank Baum and I imagined them." The critical might point out that Neill's beautiful princesses are all a little too conventionally alike, as are his handsome princes, and occasionally, like Denslow, he had difficulty in depicting a childlike child.

Although no one ages in the Land of Oz, Neill kept up with the taste of the times, as these depictions of Dorothy, above, opposite and on the next page, show. The illustration on the opposite page is from *Ozma of Oz* (1906) and above from *Dorothy and The Wizard of Oz* two years later.

Dorothy in 1916 (*Rinkitink in Oz*).

By 1921 Dorothy had begun to wear her coronet at a stylish angle (*The Royal Book of Oz*).

The Dorothy of 1928 verges toward the flapper (*The Giant Horse of Oz*).

In 1935 she adopted a languorous pose for moviegoers accustomed to glamour girls (*The Wishing Horse of Oz*).

Ozma changed with the times, too, becoming steadily more sophisticated.

1904 (*The Marvelous Land of Oz*).

1922 (*Kabumpo in Oz*).

1916 (*Rinkitink in Oz*).

1941 (*The Scalawagons of Oz*).

Neill's depiction of Glinda remained fairly constant, although she became less buxom than she appeared in *The Marvelous Land of Oz* (above).

Perhaps tiring of the same head covering, she appeared as an Egyptian in one picture in *The Patchwork Girl of Oz* (1913).

This is not to suggest that Neill's style remained constant for nearly forty years. His early Oz books, especially *The Marvelous Land of Oz*, show the influence of Denslow and the poster school of the 1890's, while the beautiful and intricate illustrations for *The Road to Oz* and *The Emerald City of Oz* suggest Rackham, Dulac and perhaps Howard Pyle. In the later Baum titles he had grown a trifle blasé about his annual task, and his drawings are simpler and occasionally somewhat careless. They are also much more humorous than his earlier work, occasionally hasty, almost always appropriate, and sometimes—at least once in every volume—very beautiful. The most serious criticism of Neill's work is that, unlike Denslow, Neill kept pace with the times. Modern readers will not object to Gibson girls or Christy girls in the earlier books, but vamps and flappers in the volumes from the 1920's are sometimes difficult to accept. However, when we find such drawings out of keeping with that nebulous thing we call "the spirit of Oz," we have to remember that it was Neill who helped create it.

The end papers for *The Royal Book of Oz* (1921) showed a galaxy of Oz characters posing for a photograph.

One illustration from *Lucky Bucky in Oz* (1942).

Two illustrations from *The Silver Princess in Oz* (1938).

Dorothy as she appeared in Jack Snow's *The Magical Mimics in Oz* (1946), illustrated by Frank Kramer.

Kramer's version of Scraps, Cap'n Bill, Trot and the Scarecrow.

Frank Kramer, who provided the pictures for Jack Snow's two Oz titles, *The Magical Mimics in Oz* and *The Shaggy Man of Oz*, tried in the first to duplicate Neill's art, submerging his own artistic personality. In the second, the pictures are more distinctively his own. *The Shaggy Man* is, in fact, an attractive volume.

"Dirk" (Dirk Gringhuis) gave *The Hidden Valley of Oz* a fresh, uncluttered look by his bold brush-and-ink technique. The pictures are a little too modern for Oz, however, and lack the detailed whimsy of Neill and Denslow.

In *Merry Go Round in Oz*, Dick Martin, having already illustrated *The Visitors from Oz* and several other peripheral Oz books, was able to experiment, blending Denslow's decorative approach and Neill's character concepts into his own cartoon-oriented style. As his own invention, he strove to develop a suitable Ozian architecture and décor—a distillation of Baroque, fairy-tale Tudor, chinoiserie and Steamboat Gothic.

It is no denigration of the artistic achievement of L. Frank Baum to suggest that a great illustrator—W. W. Denslow—and a highly skilled interpreter of fairyland —John R. Neill—helped create what readers have loved about Oz and its inhabitants for three quarters of a century. Oz, more than any other fairyland, must be seen, and we are fortunate that its illustrators have enabled us to see it so well.

Kramer was considerably more successful with Snow's *The Shaggy Man of Oz* (1949). Here are Ozma and the Shaggy Man searching magic record books in Ozma's library.

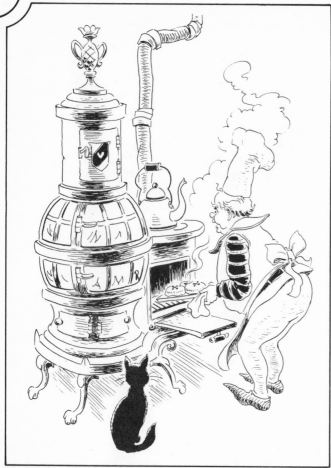

In this Dick Martin illustration from *Merry Go Round in Oz* (1963), Sir Greves is baking biscuits in a stove described by the illustrator as "a late Chippendale, early Sears, Roebuck design."

AN OZIAN DILEMMA
SCARECROW: Do we know anybody in this crowd?
TIN WOODMAN: I don't <u>think</u> so...but some of 'em look familiar.
HIPPOCAMPUS: They're all strangers to <u>me</u>!

(With apologies to Denslow, Neill, McDougall, Copelman, Hirschfeld, Kramer, Sinnickson, Ulrey, McNaught, Ruffinelli, Schulz, Maraja, et cetera.)

Dick Martin's pictorial comment on the work of various Oz illustrators appeared on the cover of an early issue of The International Wizard of Oz Club's magazine. (The "Hippocampus" is expressing what might have been Denslow's reaction to the situation.)

Dick Martin's illustration for Reilly & Lee's abridged *Ozma of Oz* (1961).

Dirk's illustrations for Rachel R. Cosgrove's *The Hidden Valley of Oz* (1951) are bold and uncluttered.

Oz
on Stage
and Screen

Chapter
4

Stone and Montgomery

Head of Ozma, posed
Vivian Reed, which w
shown at the beginning
each of L. Frank Baum's (
movies.

Frank Baum's first love was the theater. His 1882 melodrama, *The Maid of Arran*, was well received, and throughout his life he tried to repeat that success. At the turn of the century, plays tended to be boisterous, extravagant and bumptious—qualities that attracted him, as did the mechanical contrivances that made it possible to bring the magic of the fairy tale to the stage. He was also attracted by the fortunes that were being made in the theater.

In 1901 Baum and the young Chicago composer Paul Tietjens were working on ideas for stage musicals. At the same time, W. W. Denslow decided that *The Wonderful Wizard of Oz* had dramatic potential. The three men merged their plans, although the partnership was occasionally rocky, in part because Denslow, as co-owner of the book's copyright, expected a similar division of profits from the musical, even though his ultimate involvement with it was in the relatively minor role of costume designer.

Baum's original dramatic version of *The Wizard* was faithful to the book and could not have survived in the rough-and-tumble world of turn-of-the-century musical comedy. When Fred R. Hamlin, manager of the Grand Opera House in Chicago, accepted the proposal, he was interested primarily in the Scarecrow and the Tin Woodman because they had

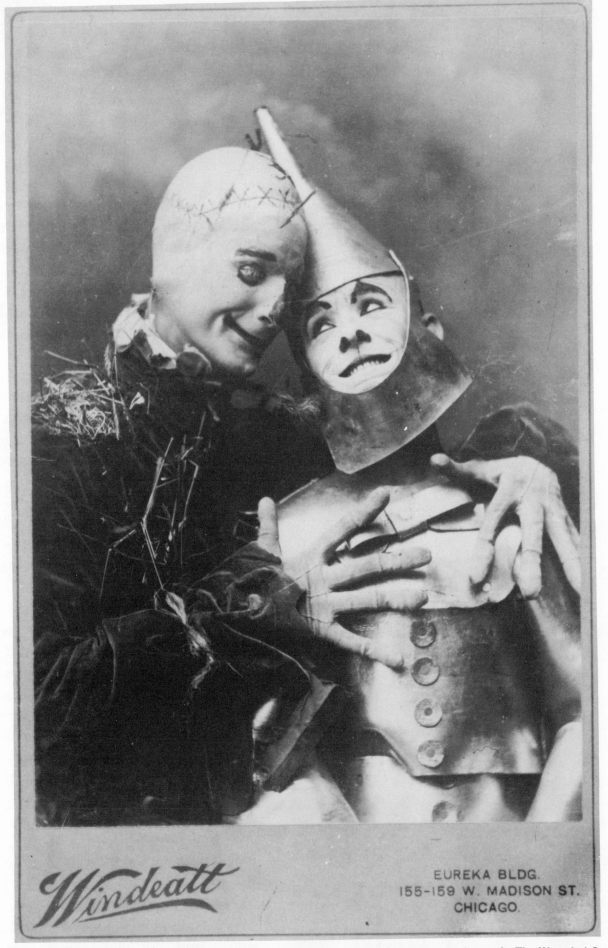

Fred Stone and David Montgomery as the original Scarecrow and Tin Man in the 1902 musical comedy, *The Wizard of Oz*.

Anna Laughlin as Dorothy.

potential as a comic team. He and Julian Mitchell, who "staged" the play (and was, in fact, in charge of nearly every aspect but the financial), realized that Baum's script would have to go. Paradoxically, the great success of the musical came in part from the fact that the revised script was poorer than the original.

Dorothy in the musical is a young lady, so that she can be the object of romantic interest. Because it is not funny to have a pet dog on stage, she is accompanied to Oz by her cow, Imogene. In the country of the Munchkins, Dorothy and Imogene are met by Cynthia Cynch, a Lady Lunatic who went mad when her lover, a woodchopper named Niccolo Chopper, disappeared; by Sir Dashemoff Daily, the poet laureate of Oz, who falls in love with Dorothy; and by Pastoria II, the rightful king of Oz, who is accompanied by a waitress named Tryxie Tryfle. Pastoria had been lured by the Wizard into his balloon which thereupon took him to Topeka, where he became a "motorman" (that is, a streetcar driver) and where he met Tryxie. The ex-king and the waitress were blown to Oz by the same cyclone that deposited Dorothy and Imogene there.

Dorothy is given a magic ring by Locasta, Good Witch of the North, and with it she brings the Scarecrow to life. A little later the two rescue the Tin Man, who turns out to be Niccolo Chopper, the Lady Lunatic's lost lover. In the meantime the Cowardly Lion has attached himself to Pastoria and Tryxie, and the two groups join forces.

Stone, Laughlin and Montgomery.

They then become trapped by the Poppy Field, played by members of the chorus disguised as giant poppies. Locasta rescues them by evoking snow to quell the lovely but deadly flowers.

At the Emerald City the Wizard's army (played by chorus girls in tights) goes through a drill, and then the Wizard puts on a performance which proves to everyone except those on stage that he is an arrant humbug: he runs swords through a basket with an obvious false bottom through which his assistant has already escaped. Dorothy, the Scarecrow, the Tin Man and Imogene enter, and the Scarecrow and the Tin Man receive their brains and heart. In the meantime Sir Wiley Gyle, a courtier whose ancestry goes back to Machiavelli, has discovered that the Wizard is a humbug and begins a counterplot to discredit both Pastoria and his successor. Eventually, after other complexities, Pastoria defeats both the Wizard and Sir Wiley, who are forced as convicts to become street cleaners. For some reason the victorious king turns against Dorothy and her friends, but as they are about to be executed, Locasta appears on the scene and saves everybody. The Tin Man and the Lady Lunatic are reunited, and Locasta promises to send Dorothy and Imogene back to Kansas.

This extraordinary plot was primarily a vehicle for irrelevant topical songs, which were interpolated throughout the musical's long run (although Tietjens is credited as composer, only a few of his songs were used);

Stone and Montgomery in *The Wizard of Oz* (1902).

The football routine.

Sir Wiley Gyle (Stephen Morley).

Top left and bottom: The Sailing routine.

displays of chorus girls in tights; wisecracks;
the high jinks of the Scarecrow and the Tin
Man; and marvelous visual effects. It was,
in fact, typical of what was called an extravaganza. The Scarecrow and the Tin Man
brought fame to the comedy team of David
Montgomery and Fred Stone. Montgomery
was an appropriately stolid Tin Man, while
Stone was an amazingly limber Scarecrow.
Scenes were later added to take advantage
of the talents of these two stars, even including a football number in which the football
looked like the Scarecrow's head.

The Wizard of Oz opened in Chicago
on June 16, 1902, to general approval,
although several reviewers criticized the plot
and various performers. Everyone praised
Montgomery and Stone and the scenic
effects. As the *Daily News* reviewer noted:

A warning to pirates from the *New York Clipper*, August 29, 1903.

A wall of *Wizard* posters at 36th Street and Fifth Avenue in New York City.

A *Chicago Tribune* cartoon of Montgomery and Stone. (Courtesy The Theatre Collection, The New York Public Library at Lincoln Center, Astor, Lenox and Tilden Foundations)

PRODUCED UNDER THE DIRECTION OF
JULIAN MITCHELL
ARD OF OZ
E POPPIES

"Money fairly drips from the gorgeous walls and skies of the Emerald City and the land of the Munchkins and from the costly robes of the pretty girls and amazing atmospheres of silver mists and golden lights."

The Wizard of Oz was a spectacular hit. It ran for fourteen weeks in Chicago and then moved to New York, opening at the new Majestic Theatre on January 20, 1903, where it ran for 293 performances to become one of the greatest successes in Broadway history up to that time. Other producers were quick to copy The Wizard; the most important imitation—and a much finer work in every respect but originality—was Victor Herbert's Babes in Toyland (1903). After its Broadway run The Wizard toured the country for most of the decade. Whatever else can be said for it, it always presented a gorgeous spectacle, slapstick comedy, and as Hamlin and Mitchell forthrightly declared in hundreds of posters and advertisements, "more pretty girls than any other show in town."

Baum was anxious to duplicate the success of The Wizard, so when he began work on The Marvelous Land of Oz, the Queer Visitors from the Marvelous Land of Oz comic page and the other Oz projects of 1904–5, he planned to climax them with a

A snowstorm saves Dorothy and her friends from the deadly poppies. Left to right: Pastoria (Owen Westford), Cowardly Lion (Arthur Hill), Tin Woodman, Dorothy, the Snow Queen (Nelly Payne), Scarecrow, Sir Dashenoff Daily (Bessie Wynn), Tryxie Tryffle (Lotta Faust) and Imogene the Cow (Joseph Schrode). (The Theatre Collection, The New York Public Library at Lincoln Center, Astor, Lenox and Tilden Foundations)

second extravaganza based on the second Oz book. That musical, *The Woggle-Bug*, opened, after several trial performances in Milwaukee, at the Garrick Theatre in Chicago on June 18, 1905.

The plot of *The Woggle-Bug* is essentially that of *The Marvelous Land of Oz*, with the addition of several extraneous subplots, including the Woggle-Bug's tendency

to fall in love with anyone wearing a certain bright plaid (borrowed from Baum's 1905 *Woggle-Bug Book*) and a romance between General Jinjur and the regent of the Emerald City. Elements that had proved successful in the *Wizard* musical were trotted out again: the Poppy Scene became a scene with the chorus dressed as sunflowers; the Wizard's shapely girl army was replaced by Glinda's shapely girl army; the comic team of the Scarecrow and the Tin Man became the comic team of Jack Pumpkinhead and the Woggle-Bug.

For understandable reasons, *The Woggle-Bug* flopped. The reviewers on the whole were not too unkind. The Chicago *Evening Post* said that it "entertained, if it did not exhilarate a large and kindly disposed crowd."

Dorothy is about to be executed. Notice the Wizard and Sir Wiley Gyle, left, as convict street cleaners. (The Theatre Collection, The New York Public Library at Lincoln Center, Astor, Lenox and Tilden Foundations)

The Wizard (Charles Swain) is confronted at the Emerald City by Pastoria and Sir Wiley Gyle. The elaborate scenery and the shapely soldiers in tights were generally admired. (The Theatre Collection, The New York Public Library at Lincoln Center, Astor, Lenox and Tilden Foundations)

The *Tribune* liked the extravaganza but called Baum's script "the weakest portion of the new offering." The well-known critic Burns Mantle was not so tactful: "It is smothered in a simplicity in which the child mind will revel, and before which the adult mind will nod." Almost everyone liked Frederic Chapin's music and two spectacles in particular: the magnification of the Woggle-Bug, which was accomplished by projecting his image on a screen, and the bombardment of the Emerald City with balloons shot from cannons. Audiences, however, stayed away from a play that was said to be merely a lifeless copy of *The Wizard of Oz* musical. The last performance was on July 12, without many of the spectacles, since the electric lights used in them had been repossessed. The cast had not been paid for some time.

Baum continued to occupy himself with plans and proposals for a multitude of theatrical projects, but the failure of *The Woggle-Bug* made producers less interested in him, and his next venture seems to have been financed in large part by himself. This was *Fairylogue and Radio-Plays,* which had a brief tour in the fall of 1908.

Fairylogue and Radio-Plays was a highly original combination of movie, lecture and magic-lantern slides. It was directed unabashedly at children, an audience Baum understood deeply and instinctively. The script and slides (both of which survive) and contemporary reviews indicate that unlike *The Wizard* and *The Woggle-Bug*, it had artistic merit. The production opened with

COMING

A FEAST OF FUN AND CARNIVAL OF BEAUTY

THE ALL NEW

WIZARD OF OZ

THE

PEERS

OF

ALL

COMIC

ARTISTS

David Montgomery

Frederick Stone

A

DUO

OF

DANCERS

WITHOUT

EQUALS

MONTGOMERY AND STONE

AND THE FAMOUS ORIGINAL COMPANY THAT TOOK NEW YORK, BOSTON AND CHICAGO BY STORM

GRAND OPERA HOUSE
ROCKFORD, ILL.

ONE NIGHT

MONDAY
JAN. 22

MORE GIRLS

AND MORE

PRETTY GIRLS

THAN EVER SEEN TOGETHER
ON THE SAME STAGE

A BATTALION OF BEAUTY-BRIGHTS
A PHALANX OF FASCINATORS
A CHALLENGE CORPS OF CHARMERS

IN THE

Wizard
OF Oz

TAKE ALL THE CHILDREN TO SEE

THE ROARING LION

AND

THE COMICAL COW

Their mad pranks and mirth-provoking pleasantries are positively without a parallel in the line of Pantomimicry

FUN!══FUN!══FUN!

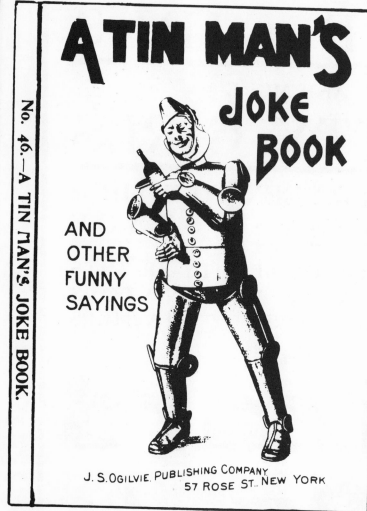

This 1904 spin-off item may have been published without the knowledge of Hamlin, Mitchell or Baum. The cover shows David Montgomery carrying a suspicious-looking bottle instead of the usual oil can. (Courtesy *The Baum Bugle*)

Baum himself entering the stage in front of a large screen on which the films and slides were shown. Baum gave a whimsical introduction explaining that he had heard of Oz from a fairy who had come to him while he was resting in a clover field. Then he stepped behind the curtain and continued to narrate while a film was projected showing him helping the various Oz characters (most of whom were played by young children) step out of a giant book. Baum's narration, which continued throughout the presentation, was the "fairylogue" portion of the program; the "radio-play" portion was the film and slides, both of which were hand-colored, supposedly by a process invented by Michel Radio (Baum's title does not use radio in its modern sense). The film and slides were apparently interspersed.

The first part of the program proper, called "The Land of Oz," consisted of scenes from *The Wonderful Wizard of Oz*, *The Marvelous Land of Oz* and *Ozma of Oz*. Then came an intermission, during which slides made from illustrations for *Dorothy and the Wizard in Oz* were projected. The second part of the program was called "John Dough and the Cherub," and consisted of an abridgment of that book. Reilly & Britton promoted the show in advertisements, and Oz books were sold in the theater.

Fairylogue and Radio-Plays premiered in Grand Rapids on September 24, 1908. From the first it was praised by reviewers, and audiences were delighted. Baum himself made an impressive figure in, as the Chicago *Record-Herald* noted, "a vanilla ice-cream

Sheet-music cover for the second Oz play (1905).

suit cut in the frock coat pattern." Not surprisingly, some reviewers compared his general appearance to that of Mark Twain.

Everyone praised the scenic effects. Early publicity indicated that the parents of young Romola Remus, who played Dorothy, refused to allow her to be in the storm scene from *Ozma of Oz* unless her life were insured heavily. Fortunately for the reputation of the older Remuses, Baum let the cat out of the bag in an interview for a long article on the production entitled "In the Fairy Land of Motion Pictures" (New York *Herald*, September 26, 1909):

"There is another illusion in my entertainment, which, however, required a good deal more ingenuity," went on Mr. Baum, "than any of these preceding things. Little Dorothy in a chicken coop is seen to be dashed about in the middle of a storm at sea with a fury almost indescribable.

"The little girl," remarked Mr. Baum, "was never at sea in her life. When I proposed this effect to the motion picture manufacturers, they laughed at me. But it was to be accomplished through a knowledge of photography. In the first place, I took motion pictures of a storm at sea.... [In the studio] I draped with dead black cloth a space in which I placed little Dorothy in her chicken coop. The coop was built on rockers which were fitted with a series of casters, and invisible wires were attached, all being concealed beneath black cloths except the coop and the child. When this was prepared I projected upon a screen at one side the picture of the sea and as the waves rolled in we made the chicken coop follow its curves and float across the black space, at the same time taking another motion picture of it upon a strip of film.

"When this strip was developed it showed the girl in the chicken coop plainly, but the dead black surrounding made the film transparent in every other part. We next

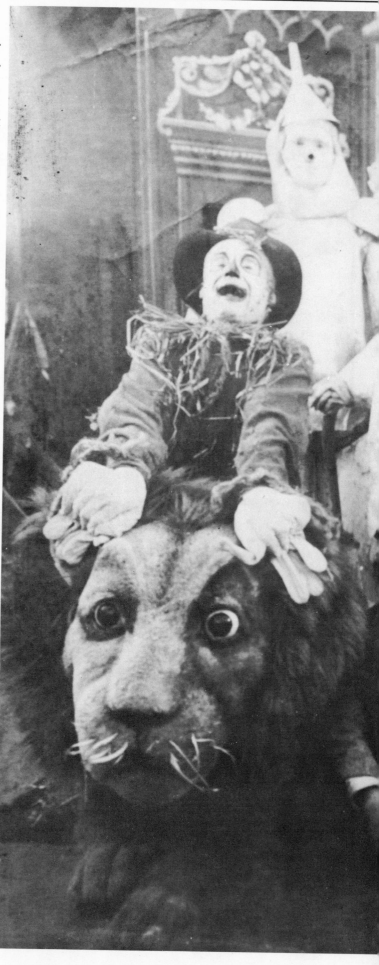

L. Frank Baum and his *Radio-Plays* actors (1908).

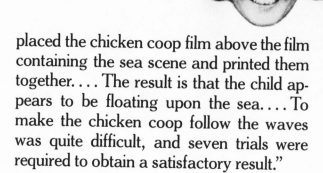

Dorothy in the *Radio-Plays* was portrayed by a child who was actually named Romolo Remus. (Courtesy Justin G. Schiller)

In this *Radio-Plays* scene, Dorothy and her three companions are easy to recognize. The strange beast with the white mane and whiskers may or may not be the Hungry Tiger.

placed the chicken coop film above the film containing the sea scene and printed them together. . . . The result is that the child appears to be floating upon the sea. . . . To make the chicken coop follow the waves was quite difficult, and seven trials were required to obtain a satisfactory result."

Fairylogue and Radio-Plays closed after its December 1908 engagement in New York City. Although it was successful with the public, Baum had not realized that sub-

stantial financial backing was needed for such a production. The debts he incurred were in a large degree responsible for his bankruptcy three years later. It was a noble experiment, one of greater significance than that flashier failure, *The Woggle-Bug*, for in *Fairylogue and Radio-Plays*, Oz was for the first time given a setting faithful to the spirit of Baum's original.

One of Baum's creditors was the Selig Polyscope Company, which had manufactured the *Radio-Plays* film. Probably as partial settlement, Selig used the film for a series of four one-reel silent movies released in 1910: *Wonderful Wizard of Oz* (apparently early episodes from the first Oz book), *Dorothy and the Scarecrow in Oz* (primarily from an adaptation of *Dorothy and the Wizard in Oz* filmed for the *Radio-Plays* but not used), *The Land of Oz* (a mélange of episodes from the first two Oz books) and *John Dough and the Cherub*. The first three one-reelers were the earliest commercially released Oz motion pictures. Otherwise little is known about them; they apparently do not survive.

Sometime around 1908 Baum began working on a dramatization of the third Oz book, *Ozma of Oz* (1907). The original title of the script seems to have been *The Rainbow's Daughter*; by the time of the revised script (which survives and is dated April 15, 1909), it was called *Ozma of Oz*. It is a very loose adaptation of the book. It begins with a storm at sea, but this time it is a girl named Betsy Bobbin, not Dorothy, who is blown off a ship; she is accompanied by Hank the Mule. A major subplot is added: the attempt of Queen Ann of Oogaboo to conquer the world (her small army with only one private is based on Ozma's army), and the rescue of the royal family of Ev is replaced by the rescue of the Shaggy Man's

The Wizard of Oz and His Irish Piglets.

L. Frank Baum Explains How His Modern Fairies Work, Aided by Ingenuity and the Camera, and Tells of the Wonderful Illusions Produced.

The Witch Preparing Her Incantation.

The Gingerbread Man Comes to Life.

Mysterious Appearance of the Little Prince.

Dorothy Preparing to Disappear.

SOMEWHERE back behind the mists of the years lies the land where fairies live, and where the aged witches do their wonderful deeds, and where beautiful princesses and handsome princes lie enchanted and come again to life, to reign over the realms which we knew so well in those other days. They seemed so clear, those castles of that dream life. The followers of the Fairy Court sat round upon their cushions of red velvet (or was it silk or satin or was it fluff?) and were wisked away by one wave of the wand by some malign old creature with ample buckles on her shoes, and that deep crowned Quaker-like hat of hers.

We knew she was a witch and we feared her, though we understood that all her powers were to be as nothing in the end, because the other one would come—the one with beautiful little wings, which were not gauzy, not downy; nor were they those of butterflies, but a dazzling, wonderful combination of all three. And so she would come and wave her wand, which would glisten with a sort of intangible, firefly effect, and straightway the little court would assemble in its place; the little king and queen would foregather upon their thrones and everybody would immediately go out into the garden.

Just as It Is in Oz.

And so Mr. Baum has his fairies from that marvellous country called Oz do

which is mysterious and electrical; we betray peevishness through instruments with holes through them and are repaid with interest by young women with large, impressive looking domes of hair at the other end of the wire. We harness nature to ease our burdens and stimulate our imaginations.

So Mr. Baum, while he honestly admits an ignorance of the processes of real fairy enchantments, as any honest but merely human person must do, thought that he might fairly use science to aid him in simulating the things which fairies really achieve. And after Mr. Baum had explained his methods to me at his rooms the other day it really became a question as to which was the more wonderful—the ingenuity with which he achieved them or that of the old witches and fairy godmothers themselves.

Pumpkin Head, whom you see (after a perilous journey into empyrean heights in a rocket) emerge from the indubitable clouds, fall clean down in front of you and then make his obeisance as if nothing had ever happened. No real witch could turn a neater trick, no godmother turning pumpkin into carriage and horses could use her art more unerringly. How is it all done? The real fairy godmothers are very unreasonable, but Mr. Baum is far more obliging, and, as the newspapers say, he is willing to tell all he knows.

"You see," said Mr. Baum to me recently, "what one might term fairy photography is something almost altogether new, and new effects have to be obtained from those which one might term the ordinary moving picture photography. Effects had to be obtained which the ordinary manipulation of the moving picture camera did not provide for—such, for instance, as magic disappearances, the changes entailed in bewitchments, scenes melting into others, sudden reappearances and so forth.

"Now, I had the idea of telling my own fairy stories to children and had the idea

dinary moving pictures consist of scenes taken from nature—a railway train coming into a station, or a steamboat, for instance, being popular things. Or brief comedies and tragedies are played before a moving film which records a number of separate incidents, which are taken so quickly that they record every phase of the action. These are positives, but when printed against another film become negatives about three-fourths of an inch high, which become projected against a screen and enlarged to, say, 12 by 16 feet at such a speed that the eye becomes deceived and they appear to move as in real life. The number of these exposures is so great, however, and the changes are so slight that it is almost impossible to tamper with them, and the presentations upon the screen are practically as the scene happened in real life.

Some of the Tricks.

"Of course, certain tricks have been commonly used in photography for a long time which are sufficiently ingenious to merit explanation and which the public have become accustomed to seeing, though generally they don't know the explanation for them. Take the boot which appears to lace itself, for instance. These effects are very laboriously arrived at by means of a number of separate exposures, with fresh arrangements and more or less long pauses between each. Thus a man will insert the lace and move away from the range of the camera, while one exposure is being taken. After this is done he will appear once more and move the lace a fraction of an inch. Again he walks away and another exposure of the camera comes—and the procedure is continued until the shoe is laced. This, you see, gives a number of separate positive exposures upon one long strip of film, all very close to one another and all component parts of the same general action. After the negative has been obtained by reprinting upon another film it is only necessary to flash it upon the screen and revolve the film rapidly to make it appear part of one movement. The long pauses between exposures are eliminated by the quickly moving strip and all appears part of one moving action. The shoe appears to lace itself. It's very simple.

"Yes, it is very simple when you understand how everything is done. Everything in life is simple when one understands it. Art is simple; only applied knowledge. So many small mechanical tricks weigh one into the other. But it makes one almost doubt the fairies. Let us hope the fairy godmothers of our youth had no way with their art.

"Another trick ... been used in ordinary moving pictures ... performances," went on Mr. Baum, ... the paper through ... agency. ...

This illustrated article about Baum's Oz motion pictures appeared in the Sunday *New York Herald* for September 26, 1909.

140

brother. Polychrome, the daughter of the rainbow, is given an important role, and both she and the Shaggy Man come from the fifth book, *The Road to Oz*, while the Rose Kingdom is based on the underground vegetable country of the Mangaboos in the fourth book, *Dorothy and the Wizard in Oz*. In fact, Baum created a new plot loosely based on *Ozma of Oz*, and in doing so, he wrote the best of his Oz theatricals.

He did not, however, find a producer until he had moved to California and met Oliver Morosco, a West Coast theater owner. In 1912, Morosco and Baum reached an agreement to produce the play, now called *The Tik-Tok Man of Oz*. It opened at Morosco's Majestic Theatre in Los Angeles on March 31, 1913, and for the first time since *The Wizard of Oz*, L. Frank Baum had a dramatic hit. After five weeks in Los Angeles, it moved to San Francisco and then to Chicago. Part of its success should be credited to Morosco's staging and to Louis F. Gottschalk's music, which is the most melodic to accompany a Baum play and is today the least dated. The Chicago reviewers recognized, of course, its similarity to the *Wizard* stage play, with its comic pair (Tik-Tok and the Shaggy Man), comic animal (Hank the Mule), girl heroine (Betsy Bobbin) and chorus girls disguised as flowers (in the Rose Kingdom). Most of them, however, were delighted; enough years had passed since *The Wizard* so that the similarity did not seem to be outrageous, as it had with *The Woggle-Bug*.

Baum had hoped that the show might go on to New York, but Morosco decided to close it that summer after its Chicago success. He was at the same time the producer of one of the greatest American stage hits of all time, and it is hardly surprising that he elected to put his energies and resources into *Peg o' My Heart*. Baum was thus free to use

FRED C. WOODWARD as Hank, the Donkey, and LEONORA NOVASIO as Betsy, in *The Tik Tok Man of Oz.* *Photograph by Terkelson and Henry, San Francisco.*

Fred C. Woodward as Hank the Mule and Leonora Novasio as Betsy Bobbin in *The Tik Tok Man of Oz* (1913).

the plot of *The Tik-Tok Man* in his 1914 O book, *Tik-Tok of Oz.*

That same year Baum decided to ente the movie business. He was living in Holly wood, the center of the nascent film industry and he was certain that the time was right fo turning extravaganzas into feature-lengtl films. The Oz Film Manufacturing Com pany was incorporated, with Baum as presi dent and Louis F. Gottschalk, who wrote the music for *The Tik-Tok Man of Oz,* a. vice-president. Both men received stock ir return for their contributions to the firm

Brochure for the Chicago performances, in October 1908 of *Fairylogue and Radio-Plays.*

L. FRANK BAUM'S FAIRYLOGUE IS ENDORSED BY PARENTS, CLERGYMEN AND EDUCATORS AS AN IDEAL ENTERTAINMENT FOR LITTLE ONES

WONDER FAIRYLOGUE TALES

Here's the Scarecrow, stuffed with straw;
The wriggliest man you ever saw.
You'll shout with laughter at the way
He capers in the Radio-Play.

ACTING RADIO-PLAY PICTURES

ACTING RADIO-PLAY PICTURES

Here's Dorothy, who travels to
The Land of Oz, the sights to view.
She meets with many a fairy fay
While wandering in the Radio-Play.

WONDER FAIRYLOGUE TALES

WONDER FAIRYLOGUE TALES

The Mitket is a merry sprite
In whom the youngsters will delight.
He's full of mischief night and day—
You'll see him in the Radio-Play.

ACTING RADIO-PLAY PICTURES

ACTING RADIO-PLAY PICTURES

The man of Tin is funny, too,
And many a laugh he'll win from you.
He may be stiff but that's his way
When acting in the Radio-Play.

WONDER FAIRYLOGUE TALES

WONDER FAIRYLOGUE TALES

The Cowardly Lion here you see,
He's not so bad's he seems to be;
You'll watch him gambol, light and gay,
Throughout the merry Radio-Play.

ACTING RADIO-PLAY PICTURES

ACTING RADIO-PLAY PICTURES

Jack Pumpkinhead's a curious sight;
His antics fill you with delight.
You'll love to see his seed-brains stray
And bungle through the Radio-Play.

WONDER FAIRYLOGUE TALES

THE ACTING PICTURES ARE PARISIAN COLOR-PHOTOGRAPHY, WONDERFULLY LIFE-LIKE, AND HAVE NEVER BEFORE BEEN SEEN IN AMERICA

FINE ARTS THEATRE
STUDEBAKER BUILDING
THE GEM OF CHICAGO'S THEATRES

MATINEES ONLY
Every Day Except Sunday at 3:30 P. M.
SATURDAY 2:30 P. M.

YOU REALLY MUST

SEE Dorothy shipwrecked at sea in a floating chicken-coop.

SEE The Gump Flying Machine soar through the air.

SEE The Gingerbread Man made and baked and brought to life.

SEE The Wooden Saw-Horse kick and prance.

SEE John Dough sail through the clouds on a sky-rocket.

SEE The Wonderful Transformations, Disappearances and Enchantments.

SEE The live Rubber Bear, the Jolly White Rabbit, the Hungry Tiger and Cowardly Lion.

SEE all the bewildering, mystical, magical scenes from Fairyland.

HEAR the quaint, merry Fairy Tales told by the author of all these wonders.

POPULAR PRICES
50c-75c and $1.00
Seats Reserved by Telephone or Mail

AN INSTANT SUCCESS

Every child should meet personally America's greatest Fairy Tale Author

L. FRANK BAUM
who has conceived and prepared this pure, sweet and wholly delightful entertainment for boys and girls of all ages. Read what the newspapers say about his

FAIRYLOGUE
in which he tells his stories in a way to hold his listeners spell-bound; and while he tells them the wonders of the

RADIO-PLAY
are unfolded, and you shout with laughter at the merry antics of all the queer characters Mr. Baum has made household favorites. Nothing more amazing than these

ACTING PICTURES
has ever been seen in America.

AUTOGRAPH MATINEE
Tuesday and Friday. Bring your favorite Baum book to be autographed by the author.

SOUVENIR MATINEE
Monday. Every child will be presented with a handsome Story Book, illustrated in colors.

THE BEST AMUSEMENT FOR CHILDREN EVER DEVISED

WONDER FAIRYLOGUE TALES

ACTING RADIO-PLAY PICTURES

John Dough's a Man of Gingerbread;
By Chick the Cherub he is led
Through strange adventures, as you'll
may
When you have seen the Radio-Play.

ACTING RADIO-PLAY PICTURES

This Tik-tok is a clock-work man,
The queerest since the world began.
You'd like to know him, and you may
If you attend the Radio-Play.

WONDER FAIRYLOGUE TALES

EVEN GROWN-UPS LOVE THIS QUAINT WONDERLAND

Verdict of Famous Critics:

"Every child must go."—*Amy Leslie in Chicago News.*

"The children squealed with delight."—*James O'Donnell Bennett in Chicago Record-Herald.*

"The Baum show is a delight."—*Percy Hammond in Chicago Post.*

"It captivated the children last night."—*O. L. Hall in Chicago Journal.*

"Mr. Baum's charming whimsicalities proved to be well worth while."—*Burns Mantle in Chicago Tribune.*

"A veritable treat for the little ones."—*Chicago Inter-Ocean.*

"A triumph of pictorial art."—*St. Louis Times.*

"Fascinating alike to old and young."—*Louise Brand in Milwaukee Sentinel.*

"The best thing to do is to take the whole family, from baby to grandma."—*St. Paul Pioneer Press.*

"Quite different, and delightfully different, from anything yet seen on the stage."—*St. Paul Dispatch.*

"There are few real entertainments for children, and this one is ideal."—*Minneapolis Journal.*

"Boys and girls will find it better fun than the circus."—*Grand Rapids Press.*

FINE ARTS THEATRE
STUDEBAKER BUILDING
THE GEM OF CHICAGO'S THEATRES

MATINEES DAILY
Beginning Saturday, Oct. 24, and continuing
FOR TWO WEEKS
3:30 to 5:15 No Evening Sat. at 2:30
Performances

The Children's Own
FAIRYLAND

America's Teller of Fairy Tales

L. FRANK BAUM
And His Wonderful
ACTING PICTURES
of
THE LAND OF OZ
and
John Dough and the **Cherub**

Two Fairy Extravaganzas
of rare beauty, presented in magnificent colors and with marvelous effects

SEATS NOW ON SALE

Sea.

Part III—Plays, Playe.

The — Times

LOS ANGELES

The Pink Sheet—Illu

TUESDAY MORNING, APRIL 1, 1913. —6 PAGES.

In the

Two of the daisies in the Field Flower Number

Burns & Fulton as "Pan" and Wood Nymph

Morton & Moore as "Tik Tok and Shaggy Man"

Chas. Ruggles as Private Files the Oogaboo army

Lenore Novasio as Betsy and Fred Woodward as "Hank"

Dolly Castles as Polychrome

Eugene Cowles as "Ruggedo" the Metal Monarch

The way it looked to "Sal."

Times artist loses beauty sleep to see first performance of Tik-Tok, but felt recompensed for loss by beauty

Some Show.

"TIK TOK" DREAM OF LOVELINESS.

BRUNTON'S GORGEOUS SCENERY BIG FEATURE.

Morton and Moore, Dolly Castles and Vera Doria Score Individual Hits—Superbly Costumed Beauty Chorus Developed by Stammers Talk of Town Today.

BY ZIP.

Of course I went to the professional performance of "The Tik Tok Man of Oz" Sunday at midnight. I also know that as a rule a prophet is without honor in his own country. But I am sure everyone in that big appreciative audience will agree with me when I say "Throw away the key, Mr. Morosco, for Tik Tok is wound up for a long run."

It is an enchanting kaleidoscope of bewildering, fairylike scenes, wonderfully costumed beauties, fascinating dances and a good old Amazon march, introducing phalanx on phalanx of shapely girls, and conjured up the days when extravaganza dominated the American stage.

The music is tuneful and musicianly. Louis F. Gottschalk composed it out of his experience as a show man, and it could not be otherwise. It is best when it is descriptive, and the storm music, which carries the prologue, is immense.

I must admit I was not so favorably impressed with the book lyrics. To be sure it formed the basis for the wonderful scenic conceptions of Robert Brunton, but there is little real sparkle. Compared with the music and the setting, the work of L. Frank Baum must take third place.

Yet it can easily be moulded into a real knockout, and I'm sure that Mr. Baum is the man to do it, for I am still laughing over the one real line he puts over:

"It is better to suffer remorse than to miss a good time." Take it from me, some mayoralty candidate is going to steal that epigram for campaign purposes.

But please do not construe me to mean that the book is not good. It

I would like to tell you about, but if I did you never would appreciate them until you saw them for yourself.

MRS. LESLIE CARTER TO APPEAR IN VAUDEVILLE.

Mrs. Leslie Carter has signed a contract to appear in vaudeville next season at a salary of $2000 a week in an act similar to that which has served as a vehicle for Amelia Bingham for many years. Mrs. Carter will appear in scenes from "Zaza," "Du Barry" and "The Heart of Maryland." Her contract with John Cort expires at the close of this season, and has not been renewed because of the impossibility to secure suitable plays for the

Imaginative.

"TIK-TOK MAN" O WHIMSICAL

BY HECTOR ALL

WHILE "The Tik-Tok Man of Oz" is based on the genial man and his monarchy, L. Frank Baum has retained about the central figure of the play all the demi-gods that his fertile imagination placed in the Olympus of the Oz.

Only one is absent from the Majestic stage—the yellow hen. The author, fully realizing the unadvisability of introducing a feminine "chantecler," omitted that great favorite.

In this he has been wiser than Rostand, whose admirable drama was better suited to reading than production on the stage.

Instead, a new character appears, one entirely unknown to the denizens of the Land of Oz.

Hank, the mule, plays admirably the part of the animal love for man and that expression of intelligence in beasts, second only to our own.

Fred Woodward, a comedian of rare merit in animal impersonations, adds a great deal to the charm of the performance by his pantomimic artistry.

Mr. Baum has devised a diversion which is an extravaganza of good taste, much sentiment, quaint with humorous irony without bitterness, which carries one to the whimsical land of imagination.

A child can understand, his parents follow with ease, the kaleidoscopic changes of characters and achievements.

Very fortunately for the enhancing of the lyric fairy play, Louis F. Gottschalk has been invited to write the musical score.

Years of practical experience, a thorough training in musical direction and composition have come to aid in the polishing of the "Tik-Tok" metal garb by a musician enamored of the possibilities of the subject.

Oliver Morosco, pontifex producer of plays, was attracted by the "Tik-Tok" magnet and gave carte blanche as to expense.

Frank Stammers staged the production with thoroughness and imaginative conception that alone would make this initial production of the play an occasion of importance.

Costumers and electricians were all drawn by Baum's magnet. Robert Brunton, to whom we owe some clever scenery in recent productions of the Morosco and Burbank theaters, was specially under the spell of the Land of Oz, in his devising of unique scenic effects.

It is seldom that a musical comedy is presented with eight changes of scenery of beautiful effects and of such great complexity.

It is difficult to really say if the wonderfully realistic "storm at sea" of the prelude, the transformation of the royal gardens, the rainbow chariot of Polychrome, the home of the field flowers or the three scenes of the metal forest are one better than the other, so different and cleverly conceived each one is, without any suggestion of effects heretofore seen.

The ingenuity and absolute novelty of the acts constitute a new contribution to scenic and electric stage effects.

In this setting of fascinating charm, Betsy Bobbin, impersonated by a little girl, Lenora Novasio, and Hank, the mule, pass through remarkable experiences. The storm wrecking the vessel and the escape of Betsy and her friend are especially realistic. Gottschalk's musical arrangement emphasizes the tempest in the orchestration of his overture.

The hothouse of the rose kingdom, which follows, introduces Frank F. Moore, well-known comedian, as The Shaggy Man, who drops from a very high and invisible apple tree in the midst of the subjects of rose kingdom clamoring for a king.

The subjects constitute a chorus of pretty, young women, selected with great discernment by Mr. Stammers. The action, however, is somewhat slow, and would be much improved by concentration of dialogue and ac-

The play, which opened in Los Angeles, received major attention on the front page of the drama section of the *Los Angeles Times*.

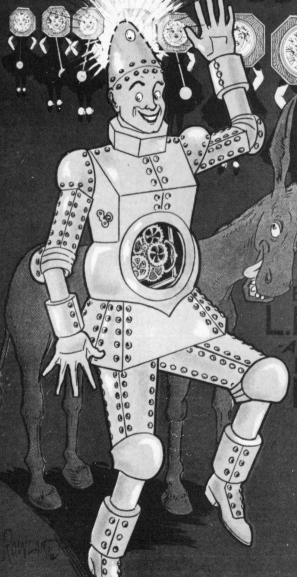

Sheet-music cover.

Baum for turning over the movie rights to his books and Gottschalk for agreeing to write original music for each film (the music was to be shipped to the various theaters and played on a piano or organ as the movie was shown). The company filed corporation papers for $100,000 and used part of its capital to purchase a seven-acre piece of land and create on it what was generally considered to be the best-equipped lot and studio in California.

The actors were almost all established performers. They included Fred Woodward, "the King of Animal Interpreters," who had played Hank the Mule in *The Tik-Tok Man*; Violet MacMillan, "the Daintiest Darling of Them All," who had played Dorothy in one of *The Wizard of Oz* road companies; Frank Moore, who had played the Shaggy Man in the 1913 musical; J. Farrell MacDonald, who was both actor and director; and the child star Mildred Harris, who some years later became the first wife of Charlie Chaplin. Hal Roach, not yet famous, played several minor parts. But Baum's chief discovery in casting the films was Pierre Couderc, a French acrobat not yet eighteen years old who was to become a leading Hollywood stunt man.

The company began filming its first movie, *The Patchwork Girl of Oz*, in June 1914, and Baum flooded the movie trade journals with advertisements and publicity for it. *The Patchwork Girl* featured Couderc in the title role and Violet MacMillan as Ojo. The plot is very close to the book, with the addition of a subplot about the love of Dr. Pipt's daughter, Jesseva, for a Munchkin

The two principal characters in *The Tik Tok Man of Oz*, Tik Tok and the Shaggy Man, were portrayed by Frank Moore and James Morton, but the two unknowns, above, who played Queen Ann Soforth and Private Files—Charlotte Greenwood and Charlie Ruggles—were the two destined for later fame.

MAJESTIC THEATRE

Grand Circle, Broadway and 59th Street.

NEW YORK'S FINEST—THE WORLD'S SAFEST THEATRE.
POSITIVELY FIREPROOF—42 EXITS.

F. D. STAIR and A. L. WILBUR,	- - - -	Proprietors
GEO. H. NICOLAI,	- - - -	General Manager
JOHN S. FLAHERTY,	- - - -	Manager

WARNING.—Tickets purchased from speculators on sidewalk WILL POSITIVELY BE REFUSED AT THE DOOR. Patrons will confer a favor on the management, and at the same time can serve the interests of the public, by refusing to deal with speculators. IF YOU DO NOT BUY THEIR TICKETS they must abandon the business.

LADIES! SPECIAL NOTICE!! Use the Hat Holder, which you will notice on the back of every other Seat. Your hat pin goes through the hole in the holder.

CARRIAGE ENTRANCE, 59TH ST.   **CARRIAGE EXIT, 58TH ST.**

WEEK COMMENCING MONDAY EVENING, MARCH 21, 1904

Evenings at 8.   Wednesday and Saturday Matinees at 2.
Wednesday Matinees, Popular Prices.

SAFEST THEATRE IN THE WORLD.
LOWEST FIRE INSURANCE RATE OF ANY THEATRE IN NEW YORK.

FRED R. HAMLIN Presents

THE WIZARD OF OZ

MUSICAL EXTRAVAGANZA.

Book and Lyrics by L. Frank Baum. Music by Paul Tietjens and A. Baldwin Sloane.
The Entire Production arranged and staged by JULIAN MITCHELL.

LIST OF CHARACTERS.
(Arranged in the order of their entrance upon the stage)

ACT I.

SCENE 1—A Kansas Farm.
(Painted by Fred Gibson from designs by Walter W. Burridge.)

Dorothy Gale, a Kansas girl, the victim of a cyclone................Anna Laughlin
The Cow, named Imogene, Dorothy's playmate ....Joseph Schrode
Golfman ....Geo. Fields
Farm Hands............Misses Fisher, Donalson, Burnell, Von Brune, Costello, Townsend, Moffatt, Gerard, Diamond, Wilton, Arnold. Messrs. Christian, Cleveland, Devlin, Young.

SCENE 2—(Transformation)—The Country of the Munchkins.
(Painted by John Young.)

Tommie Top.............		Anna Fitzhugh
Peter Pop		Elizabeth Young
Simon Slick		Emily Fulton
Antonia	Munchkins	Sadie Emmons
Sophronia		Ella Gilroy
Premonia		Lillian De Vere
Malvonia		Stubby Ainscoe
Semponia		Josephine Clayton

Munchkin Youths......Misses Clara Selton, May Du Frene, May Gunderman, M. De Vere, Emma Clark, Nellie Lane, Helen Turner, Virginia Kendall, Osia Thompson. Messrs. Steele, Bingham, Diskins, Hoskins, Nichols, West.
Munchkin Maidens......Marie Mathey, Anna Leslie, Laura Young, Minna Doerge, Edna Leach, Nancy Crawford, Lola Gordon, Nellie Payne, Beatrice Gilbert.
Cynthia Cynth, the lady lunatic, a Munchkin maiden................Allene Crater
The Witch of the North, a friend in need................Albertina Benson
Sir Dashemoff Daily, Poet Laureate...........................Bessie Wynn
The Army of Pastoria..Earl Dewey
Pastoria II., ex-king of the Emerald City, with a conspiracy to regain his throne................Owen Westford
Tryxie Tryfle, prospective Queen of the Emerald City................Lotta Faust
Brigadier-General Riskitt, commanding Pastoria's army .... Harold P. Morey
The Scarecrow, looking for brains..........................Fred A. Stone

SCENE 3—The Road through the Forest.
(Painted by John Young.)

The Cowardly Lion ....Arthur Hill
Nick Chopper the Tin Woodman, in search of a heart........David C. Montgomery
Sir Wiley Gyle, a conspirator who scorns all magical arts............Stephen Maley

SCENE 4—The Poppy Field.
(Painted by John Young.)

The Poppy Queen ....Josephine Clayton
Poppy Flowers........ Misses Moffatt, Fisher, Townsend, Leslie, Leach Gunderman. Gerard, Dean, Clark, Von Brune, Lane, Gilbert, Diamond, Burnell, Gordon, Selton, Young, Blye, Kendall, Diamond, Du Frene, Costello, Arnold, Thompson, Doerge, Donalson

SCENE 5—(Transformation)—The Poppy Field in Winter.
(Painted by John Young.)

Snow Queen.............		Nellie Payne
		Ella Gilroy
		Lillian De Vere
Snow Boys,		Marie Mathey
		Anna Fitzhugh
		Emily Fulton
		Elizabeth Young
Snow Girls,		Sadie Emmons
		M. De Vere
		Helen Wilton

ACT II.

SCENE—The Courtyard of the Wizard's Palace.
(Painted by Walter Burridge.)

Leo, Captain of the Relief Guards................George B. Fields
Captain of the Patrol....................................Sadie Emmons
The Patrol........Misses Gerard, Lane, Donalson, Dean, Thompson, Costello, Gunderman, Arnold, Diamond, Von Brune, Clark, Kendall, Fisher, Turner.
Alonzo, the Wizard's Confederate................Earl Dewey

Silleus .... , ...		H. Devlin
Sophocles................	The	F. Kelsey
Pericles................	Wizard's Wise Men,	Irving H. Christian
Diogenes................		Chas Hoskins

Bardo, the Wizard's factotum ....Ella Gilroy
Oz, the Wonderful Wizard, Past Master of Magic, ruler of the Emerald City and Potentate of the Land of Oz................Charles Swain

ACT III.

SCENE 1—The Borderland, Dividing the Kingdom of Oz from the Dominions of the Good Witch. (Painted by John Young.)

Alberto, Officer of the Day.........................Sadie Emmons

WAITRESSES.		COOKS.	
Gloriana Jane........	Nancy Crawford	Claude Cliquot.........	Nellie Payne
Violet Victoria.........	M. De Vere	Alphonse Fripon.........	Osie Thompson
Gladys Ann	Ella Gilroy	Marcel Moreau........	Stubby Ainscoe
Leontine Em............	Emily Fulton	Louis Le Beau........	Vernon Arnold
Vera Ellen...........	Lillian De Vere	Francois Giblets	May Du Frene
Aileen Nance	Anna Fitzhugh	Jean De Char........	Anna Fitzhugh
Pansy Lil.........	Josephine Clayton	Remnante Saute	Marie Clayton
Lavinia Loo	Lola Gordon	Pungue De Sert	Edna Leach
Lau dresses		Misses Gilbert, Gunderman, Burnell, Wilton Thompson,	

Von Brune, Costello, Doerge, Leslie, Mathey, Moffatt, Fisher.
Royal Guards ....Misses Townsend, Turner, Donalson, Kendall, Selton, Diamond, Young, Gerard, Dean, Clark, Lane.

SYNOPSIS OF MUSIC.
Musical Director, CHARLES ZIMMERMAN.

ACT I.

1. Opening—"Life in Kansas" (Tietjens)
2. "Niccolo's Piccolo" (MacDonough and Sloan)....................Cynthia
3. "The Tale of the Cassowary" (Cobb and Edwards)................Cynthia
4. Duet—"Down on the Brandywine" (Bryan and Mullen)........Trixie and Pastoria
5. "Carry Barry" (MacDonough and Sloan)........................Dorothy
6. "Alas for the Man Without Brains" (Baum and Tietjens)........Scarecrow
7. "I Love You all the Time" (W. Anderson)....................Sir Daily
8. "Mary Canary" (Moran and Furth)............................Sir Daily
9. "When You Love, Love, Love" (Baum and Tietjens), Scarecrow, Tin Woodman and Dorothy
10. "Poppy Chorus" (Baum and Tietjens)

ACT II.

11. "The Tale of the Red Shirt" (Brackett and Medor)............The Wizard
12. "It's Enough to Make a Perfect Lady Mad" (Bryan and Mullen)....Cynthia
13. Medley—"Dance of All Nations" (Smith and Sloan).
    a "Connemara Christening"....................................Wizard
    b "Good-bye, Fedora" (O'Dea and Adams)......................Scarecrow
    c "Wee Highland Mon" ....Tin Woodman
    d "Under a Panama" (Bryan and Mullen)........................Dorothy
    e Dance—"An Afternoon Tea"........Scarecrow, Tin Woodman and Dorothy
14. "Johnnie, I'll Take You" (Cobb and Edwards)..................Trixie
15. "I Never Loved a Love as I Love You" (Cobb and Edwards)......Sir Daily
16. Duet—"The Nightmare" (Bryan and Mullen) ....Scarecrow and Tin Woodman
17. "I'd Like to go Halves in That"........Scarecrow and Tin Woodman
18. Finale

ACT III.

19. "The Traveler and the Pie" (Baum and Tietjens)..............Scarecrow
20. "Must You"...Tin Woodman
21. "The Sweetest Girl in Dixie" (O'Dea and Adams)..............Dorothy

The Fancy Costumes designed by MRS. EDWARD SIEDLE, and the Character Costumes by W. W. Denslow (illustrator of the book) were executed by Mrs. E. Castel-Bert. Poppy Hats by Charles Joseph. Wigs by Wm. Hepner & Co. Shoes by Alston. Scenery built by P. J. McDonald. Properties by Edward Siedle. Electrical Effects by Kliegl Bros.

Executive Staff for "THE WIZARD OF OZ" Company.

Manager...		W. M. Gray
Stage Director.......................................		Charles Mitchell
Assistant Stage Manager.............................		Irving Christian

Program for the New York City production of *The Wizard of Oz.*

Two Old Favorites

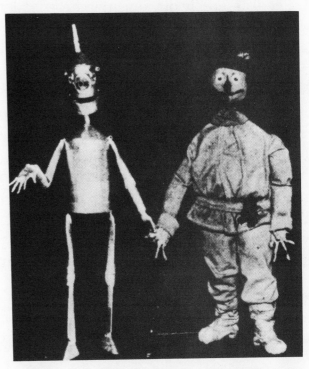

THE MOVING PICTURE WORLD 1737

Above are Nick Chopper, the well-known Tin Woodman of Oz, and his boon companion, the Scarecrow, as Jean Gros has fashioned them for his Marionette performance of "The Land of Oz," now touring the United States. An idea of the size of Oz Marionette play is given by the cast of characters and interesting program printed below.

BE SURE TO SEE THE WHIMSICAL "WOOZY" and all the other queer, quaint characters in

The Patchwork Girl of Oz

Released through the PARAMOUNT PROGRAM
SEPTEMBER 28th, 1914

It's a whirlwind of laughter, pathos and illusion

Make Arrangements Now to Book

The Magic Cloak of Oz

Our second big feature just completed. Featuring VIOLET MACMILLAN, "the daintiest darling of them all," and FRED WOODWARD, the King of Animal Personators.

Make your crowded houses laugh with OZ FEATURES. Every scene full of real heart interest and genuine comedy.

The Oz Film Manufacturing Co.

Studio and Laboratories
Santa Monica Blvd., from Gower to Lodi Sts.
Los Angeles, California

An advertisement from *The Moving Picture World* for September 29, 1914.

Jean Gros' Marionettes, present

"THE MAGICAL LAND OF OZ"

A Puppet Play by Ruth Plumly Thompson
Music composed and arranged by Irene Griffin Gros.
Additional numbers by Norman Sherrerd.
Lyrics by Ruth Plumly Thompson.

Characters:

Dorothy, who lives in Kansas	Queen Ozma of OZ
Aunt Em	Ruggedo, the Gnome King
Tik-Tok of Oz.	Kaliko, his chief Steward
Uncle Henry	Tik-Tok Machine Man
Toto, the pup	Soldier with the Green
The Scarecrow	Whiskers
The Tin Woodman	Giant Horse of OZ
The Cowardly Lion	Leader of the Orchestra
The Patchwork Girl	

Also Gnomes, birds, snakes, rabbits, etc.
Feature characters appearing in the Emerald City:

The Juggler	The Magician
Clown and Donkey and	The Tenny Wenny Dancers
Balloon	Showman, Director of the
Trapeze Man	Emerald City Puppets
Ball Walker	

and
THE FIFTEEN-PIECE OZ ORCHESTRA
* * * * *

Scenes of the Play

Prologue. Scene 1. Woodland Glade in Oz.
Scene 2. The Magic Ship.
Scene 3. Princess Languidere's throne room.
Scene 4. The Gnome King's Cavern.
Scene 5. The Carnival in the Emerald City.

Promotion for the nation-wide tour of Jean Gros' Marionettes (1928).

lad named Danx. The movie is noteworthy for its trick photography, especially the magical assembly of the dismembered Patchwork Girl. Like the other feature movies produced by the Oz film company, it was in five reels.

Baum and his associates were excited by the movie and expected to have little difficulty distributing it. But finding a distributor in a period when most of the large theaters were owned or controlled by the major producers was difficult. Finally Paramount agreed to distribute the film, and it was officially released on September 28, 1914. Reviewers liked it, and several compared it to a musical extravaganza. The company promoted it as such. There was, of course, a group of soldiers played by chorus girls in tights, and one reviewer pointed out for older members of the audience that "There is a wealth of pretty girls,

Officers of the Oz Film Manufacturing Company (1914-15). Left to right: Clarence Rundel, Secretary; L. Frank Baum, President; H.M. Walderman, Treasurer; Louis F. Gottschalk, Vice-President.

as many as ever were gathered in one picture, and it may candidly be said they are not all timid about displaying their charms."

Everyone, in fact, liked the picture except audiences. They stayed away in droves, and those who did attend complained that despite the love interest Baum had added to the film, it was childish. The first feature film about Oz—made by L. Frank Baum himself—flopped.

Before *The Patchwork Girl of Oz* was released, the company had completed its second film, *The Magic Cloak of Oz*, and begun its third, *His Majesty, the Scarecrow of Oz*. *The Magic Cloak of Oz* has nothing to do with Oz; it is a dramatization of Baum's 1905 fantasy *Queen Zixi of Ix*. After the failure of *The Patchwork Girl*, Paramount refused to distribute *The Magic Cloak* or any other productions of the Oz film company. *The Magic Cloak* was finally released in 1917 by the National Film Corporation, two years after its producers went out of business.

It is likely that the Oz film company did not push *The Magic Cloak* after Paramount had rejected it. Instead it concentrated its energies on the elaborate *His Majesty, The Scarecrow of Oz*. The movie is a hodgepodge of material that Baum later used to much better advantage in his book *The Scarecrow of Oz*, but it has a number of striking cinematic effects—Old Mombi the witch being sealed in a tin can, underwater scenes, a Wall of Water, the Scarecrow being carried off by a man-sized crow, and most impressive of all, the freezing of Princess Gloria's heart.

Two stills from *The Patchwork Girl of Oz*, showing Scraps the Patchwork Girl, played by Pierre Couderc, a French acrobat,

and the Woozy, played by Fred C. Woodward.

152

Stills from *His Majesty, The Scarecrow of Oz.*

PRESERVED WITCH

"If I let you out, will you melt the heart of Princess Gloria?"

The Oz Film Manufacturing Company put on a premiere performance in Los Angeles on October 5, 1914. Reviews were good, but the word had spread; no distributor was interested. In desperation the company decided to capitalize on the reputation of *The Wizard of Oz* musical and advertised it bluntly (and falsely) as a "Photo-Extravaganza" of that work. Finally, in January 1915, the Alliance Films Corporation agreed to release the movie, and it appeared in February as *The New Wizard of Oz.* It was still being shown under that title as late as 1920.

Alliance's agreement to release the movie was part of a general arrangement it had reached with Baum and his associates whereby Alliance would choose all the future features that the company would produce; and Alliance made it clear that its choices would not include fairy-tale extravaganzas. Late in 1914 the Oz company released its actors. Other producers rented portions of its lot and studio, including Famous Players, which filmed a Mary Pickford movie there. In March 1915, however, the Oz company reopened to film *The Gray Nun of Belgium,* an adult feature on the European war. Frank J. Baum, L. Frank Baum's eldest son, was now in charge; in order to escape the reputation the Oz Film Manufacturing Com-

pany had gained during the previous year, he changed its name to Dramatic Features Company. For some unknown reason Alliance, which had approved *The Gray Nun*, refused to distribute it, and that was the deathblow for the company. For several more months it rented out its lot before giving up its charter in the summer of 1915.

The Oz Film Manufacturing Company was probably Baum's most spectacular dramatic failure, although this time he had invested no money. It seems to have failed because extravaganzas were no longer so popular, because its films did not appeal to adult tastes and because in an age of rapid cinematic advances (D. W. Griffith's *Birth of a Nation* appeared only a year after the Oz film company went out of business), Baum's films, for all their clever effects, were old-fashioned.

In 1916 Baum was involved in plans for a never-produced *Snow White* musical with sets by Maxfield Parrish, but his 1914 Oz films were his last real dramatic fling.

After Baum's death there was for some years considerably less interest in dramatic adaptations of Oz. The 1925 silent-movie version of *The Wizard of Oz*, produced by Chadwick Pictures as a vehicle for the comic Larry Semon, who played the Scarecrow and directed the film, is most interesting today because it featured as the Tin Woodman Oliver Hardy, before he and Stan Laurel became a team. The plot is not easy to follow. It opens with a little girl dreaming about *The Wizard of Oz*, although her dream is quite different from any book the

"From Brain to Screen"

OZ FILMS are DISTINCTIVE. No rehash of worn-out plays, inane magazine stories or discarded novels, but ORIGINAL Creations of the World's Greatest Living Author of Fairy Tales, L. FRANK BAUM, who has infused **OZ FILMS** with the rich, red blood of his imaginative genius.

Clean and wholesome, teeming with *Romance, Comedy* and *Adventure,* **OZ FILMS** are transferred direct FROM BRAIN TO SCREEN, with all their wealth of Illusions, Marvels, Transformations, Legend, Love and Laughter. **EFFECTS NEVER BEFORE SEEN ON THE SCREEN** *— never before attempted by any producer.*

❧ MULTIPLE REEL FEATURES, released whenever our Master Producers consider them as nearly perfect as modern film craft can make them. ❧ A full musical score composed by Louis F. Gottschalk to fit the action, is furnished free with each picture.

Watch for further announcements

OZ FILMS are produced under the personal supervision of Mr. L. FRANK BAUM.

The Oz Film Manufacturing Co.

Santa Monica Boulevard from Gower to Lodi Sts.
Los Angeles, California

One of the most entertaining children's pictures of all time that grown-ups will equally enjoy.

Advertisements for the 1925 silent movie, featuring Larry Semon as the Scarecrow. A comparative unknown, Oliver Hardy, played the Tin Woodman.

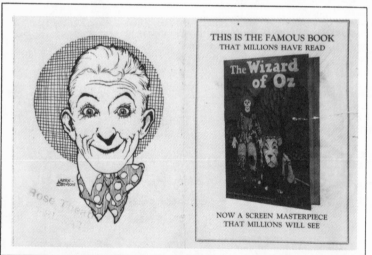

THIS IS THE FAMOUS BOOK THAT MILLIONS HAVE READ

The Wizard of Oz

NOW A SCREEN MASTERPIECE THAT MILLIONS WILL SEE

IT'S NEW! IT'S NOVEL!

THE
WIZARD
OF OZ
THE ALL STAR CAST

LARRY SEMON .... as .. The Scarecrow
BRYANT WASHBURN .. " .. Prince Kynde
DOROTHY DWAN ...... " .. Dorothy
VIRGINIA PEARSON ... " .. Countess Vishuss
CHARLIE MURRAY ..... " .. The Wizard
OLIVER HARDY .... " .. The Tin Woodman
JOSEF SWICKARD ..... " .. The Prime Minister
MARY CARR .... " .. Dorothy's Mother
G. HOWE BLACK ...... " .. Rastus

Over a million copies of the book sold in the past 24 years.

A Famous Stage Play Made Into A Photoplay Masterpiece

SEE!
The Cyclonic Kansas Tornado and Whirlwind
The Den of Ferocious Man Eating Lions
The Thrilling Airplane Rescue and Leap for Life.
Thrills! Stunts! Smiles! Laughter

A Treat for Kids from 6 years to 60

viewers might have read. It seems that Dorothy, a young lady played by Semon's wife, Dorothy Dwan, is really a princess of Oz and the heir to the throne. She had been kidnapped as a baby and sent to Kansas. Dorothy and two farm hands, played by Semon and Hardy, are blown by cyclone to Oz, along with Rastus, played by an actor with the regrettable name of G. Howe Black. While there, Semon and Hardy disguise themselves as a Scarecrow and a Tin Man to avoid capture. The rest of the film is filled with tedious Graustarkian adventures until the usurper is driven from the throne and Dorothy becomes Queen of Oz. The Wizard himself has a minor role as a sort of humbug court magician. The scenario is credited to "L. Frank Baum, Jr." (i.e., Frank Joslyn Baum) and Leon Lee. The movie failed, and although prints of it survive, it is known chiefly from the 1925 Bobbs-Merrill "photoplay" edition of *The Wizard* illustrated with stills.

Beginning in 1928, Jean Gros's French Marionettes toured the country with a "marionette extravaganza with music" entitled *The Magical Land of Oz* by the then Royal Historian, Ruth Plumly Thompson. It was in part a very free adaptation of *Ozma of Oz*. The marionettes themselves were elaborate, including a fourteen-piece puppet orchestra. Also during the late 1920's the distinguished director Ellen Van Volkenburg presented a marionette dramatization of *The Wizard of Oz* in various theaters. Professor Edward Wagenknecht, who saw it in Seattle, con-

We are now Releasing Territorial Rights on our Five-Reel Feature, Adapted from L. Frank Baum's Famous Musical Comedy

"THE WIZARD OF OZ"

As is generally well known, the musical comedy "The Wizard of Oz," played for eight years without ever missing a performance. As a result, millions of people all over this country are familiar with its quaint characters and the queer country in which the story is laid.

The announcement that the OZ FILM COMPANY was about to release this well known play brought a swarm of eager inquiries from exchanges and exhibitors throughout the country. After careful consideration of the matter the company decided to release this five-reel picture direct, believing it is too big a proposition to place on any "program," no matter how good.

Over two-thirds of the United States and Canada have been contracted for to date. The remaining territory is moving fast and present indications are that within 30 days the entire country will be covered.

❧ ❧ ❧

"A man or woman can sit through 'The Wizard of Oz' and get more real enjoyment out of the extravaganza than from many pretentious dramas."—*Motion Picture News.*

❧ ❧ ❧

"In 'The Wizard of Oz,' L. Frank Baum has found a region of quips and quirks, a place so full of whimsical abandonment that adults will give themselves up to the illusion of its fairy land."—*Motion Picture News.*

❧ ❧ ❧

The Cast of Characters

DOROTHY, a Kansas girl who is wandering in the Land of Oz..........VIOLET MACMILLAN
The Scarecrow.....................Frank Moore
The Tin Woodman.................Pierre Couderc
The Cowardly Lion................Fred Woodward
King Krewel.....................Raymond Russell
Googly-Goo, a wealthy courtier......Arthur Smollet
The Wizard of Oz.................J. Charles Hayden
Pon, the Gardener's Boy............Todd Wright
Princess Gloria, niece to King Krewel..Vivian Reed
Old Mombi, the Witch...............Mai Wells
Button-Bright, who is lost and doesn't care....
..................................Mildred Harris

Mr. Woodward also personates the Kangaroo, the Crow, the Cow and the Mule.

The production is directed by J. Farrell Macdonald.

Cinematography by James A. Crosby.

Original "Dorothy" in the Musical Comedy of "The Wizard of Oz" is Cast as "Dorothy" in This Film

VIOLET MACMILLAN

As "Dorothy" in "The Wizard of Oz"

Miss MacMillan played "Dorothy," in the "Wizard of Oz" Company organized by Hurtig & Seaman.

The Famous "Scarecrow" and the "Tin Woodman" Appear in Pictures

We have the SCARECROW, as wobbly and lovable as when Fred Stone tumbled around the stage; the TIN WOODMAN brought back to life after the manner of Dave Montgomery's excellent impersonation; the WIZARD himself; little DOROTHY, the COWARDLY LION and others. In fact we have put into motion pictures that well-beloved musical comedy, "THE WIZARD OF OZ," so that its millions of friends from the days of its stage success can once again enjoy the story and action that has delighted them so thoroughly in the past.

The scenario is, of course, by Mr. L. Frank Baum, the famous author of all the Oz stories. He has given his entire time to this production and has turned out a masterpiece of film-craft. The subject is 4700 feet in length and no expense was spared in making the production. In fact, it cost over $20,000.00—about $4000 a reel.

The picture is full of trick camera work, wonderful illusions and genuine comedy, and while it is written and interpreted to the adult standard, it also holds a special appeal for children who love its quaint characters.

Mombi Loses Her Head

Advertising Accessories for "The Wizard of Oz"

A complete line of handsome accessories has been prepared to assist the exchanges and exhibitors on this picture.

Paper, handsomely lithographed in four colors, with permanent inks and paper, is supplied in two subjects of one sheets; two subjects of three sheets; two subjects of six sheets.

Sets of stills—sixteen to a set—come in beautiful hand-colored prints. Advance slides; heralds; electrotypes and advertising cuts are also furnished at small cost.

In addition to this, the OZ FILM MANUFACTURING COMPANY maintains an advertising bureau where exchanges and theaters may at all times secure assistance in preparing advertising matter and publicity, free of charge.

The Tin Woodman Drives Away Mombi, the Wicked Witch

158

Keystone Comedy veteran Charlie Murray mugged his way
through the 1925 film as the humbug wizard, shown here
performing an improved version of the rabbit-out-of-a-hat trick.

Jell-O, which sponsored the Oz radio show, used Oz characters to promote its product.

In the 1925 film, as in the 1939 MGM version, the Scarecrow and the Tin Woodman appear first as Kansas farmhands. Dorothy was coyly played by Dorothy Dwan, Larry Semon's wife.

Hardy, Dwan and Semon in Oz.

siders it "the only really faithful and satisfying production of any of Baum's works that I have ever seen." That opinion by an important critic makes us regret that we know very little about the Van Volkenburg version of *The Wizard*.

The first animated cartoon version of *The Wizard of Oz* was produced in early 1933 by Ted Eshbaugh, a pioneer in animation. His Oz cartoon was one of the earliest to be in color and to have a full sound track, but legal difficulties prevented it from being released during the 1930's, and it apparently has not been released since. Prints, however, are known to survive.

While very few have seen the Eshbaugh cartoon, many remember nostalgically another project of the 1930's: the Jell-O *Wizard of Oz* radio show. Through agreement with Reilly & Lee and Mrs. Baum, Jell-O sponsored a fifteen-minute program based on the Baum Oz books every Monday, Wednesday and Friday from 5:45 to 6 P.M. on NBC. The program was broadcast for the first time on September 25, 1933, and for the last on March 23, 1934, at which time Jell-O decided to sponsor Jack Benny instead. The show starred Nancy Kelly, then twelve years old, as Dorothy. Surviving scripts indicate that the action continued from episode to episode and that it was a strange mishmash of Baum stories. The episode for March 12, for example, included in fifteen minutes Johnny Dooit (from *The Road to Oz*), the Phanfasms (from *The Emerald City of Oz*) and burial in popcorn snow (from *The Scarecrow of Oz*). Frank Novak composed all the music for the show and conducted it on a four-piece orchestra. As premiums, Reilly & Lee reprinted for Jell-O four of the *Little Wizard* stories, each with a drawing on the back cover of the Scarecrow and the Tin Woodman carrying a giant dish of Jell-O and with recipes following the story.

Nancy Kelly and her co-performers broadcasting an episode of the 1933-34 *Wizard of Oz* radio show. (Courtesy The National Broadcasting Company, Inc.)

ROYAL MANAGEMENT of OZ
ANNOUNCES
JEAN GROS' FRENCH
MARIONETTES

IN A MARIONETTE EXTRAVAGANZA WITH MUSIC
"THE MAGICAL LAND of OZ"
BY
RUTH PLUMLY THOMPSON
FOUNDED ON THE FAMOUS STORIES BY L. FRANK BAUM

FOR ENGAGEMENTS ADDRESS ALL COMMUNICATIONS TO
H. J. RUPERT MANAGEMENT
JEAN GROS' FRENCH MARIONETTES
1125 KNICKERBOCKER BUILDING
NEW YORK CITY

Then came the 1939 Metro-Goldwyn-Mayer version of *The Wizard of Oz*, one of the best-loved and most lucrative movies of all time. The Baum family had sold the movie rights to Samuel Goldwyn in 1934, and he resold them to M-G-M's Arthur Freed. Eventually Mervyn LeRoy became producer and Freed associate producer. Production began in 1938, and the finished movie premiered at Grauman's Chinese Theatre in Hollywood on August 15, 1939. The story of the production has often been told, how M-G-M first wanted Shirley Temple to play Dorothy, how Buddy Ebsen was first cast as the Tin Woodman but developed a severe reaction to his metallic make-up, how "The Jitterbug" musical sequence was cut out at the last minute, how "Over the Rainbow" nearly suffered the same fate, how the movie made a star of Judy Garland. Here we want to make only a few comments on the picture as a movie rather than as a legend and an annual institution on television.

With the possible exception of the Van Volkenburg puppet show, the 1939 movie was better than any earlier adaptation. The cast is excellent: Ray Bolger is as fine a Scarecrow as was Fred Stone; Bert Lahr, with his exaggerated Bronx accent, is a superb Cowardly Lion; Margaret Hamilton's Wicked Witch is one of the great delights of the movie; Jack Haley as the Tin Woodman is suitably sentimental; and Judy Garland's interpretation of Dorothy is utterly believable in its wistfulness. The film suffers, however, from making the entire Oz sequence a dream; the final product is too slick; and the ending

The Wiz: Hinton Battle, Stephanie Mills, James Wigfall, Tiger Haynes. (© Martha Swope)

("There's no place like home") too senti-mental. Billie Burke, one of the screen's great portrayers of scatter-brained ladies, is completely miscast as Glinda. But the movie is nonetheless one of the finest of all film fantasies and has influenced most later Oz dramatizations. For many today, Oz is not Baum but Judy Garland, Ray Bolger, Bert Lahr, and Margaret Hamilton—and that's not necessarily bad.

The film was highly successful when it was first released and was successfully re-released in 1949. On December 25, 1950, the *Lux Radio Theatre* presented an adaptation with Judy Garland. A 1955 rerelease was unsuccessful. Then, in 1956, the movie was leased to CBS for television and began its noteworthy second career. CBS broadcast the film in 1956, every year from 1959 through 1962 and 1964 through 1967, and again in 1976; NBC broadcast the film every year from 1968 through 1974. Its television appearances have meant that more people have seen the Metro-Goldwyn-Mayer *Wizard of Oz* than any other movie.

It is surprising that there were no significant Oz adaptations from 1939 until 1960, although there was very nearly a Walt Disney film. In the mid-1950's Disney purchased the theatrical rights from the Baum family to the later Baum Oz books and in 1957 announced that filming would commence that November on *The Rainbow Road to Oz*. It was to feature actors and actresses rather than animations, and apparently several of the television Mouseketeers were to have starring roles. For reasons unknown, the movie was never completed.

On September 18, 1960, the *Shirley Temple Show* presented a one-hour adaptation of *The Land of Oz* on NBC. It was the first adaptation intended specifically for television, and the first important Oz dramatization since the M-G-M movie. *The Land of Oz* starred Shirley Temple as Tip and Ozma, Ben Blue as the Scarecrow, Sterling Holloway as a wistful Jack Pumpkinhead, and Agnes Moorehead as a villainous Mombi with a Cockney accent. New characters were the wicked Lord General Nikidik (Jonathan Winters) and his servant, Graves the butler (Arthur Treacher). The show was repeated on NBC on April 2, 1961. Shirley Temple's *Land of Oz* was well-scripted and well-acted; it should be shown again.

The Land of Oz television adaptation was the beginning of a flood of Oz dramatizations. *The Wizard* has been featured in the *Ice Capades* (1960); Mardi Gras in New Orleans (1971); a traveling fashion show (1964); an underwater feature at

Ben Blue as the Scarecrow, Shirley Temple as Tip, Sterling Holloway as Jack Pumpkinhead in the 1960 television production of *The Land of Oz*. (Courtesy The National Broadcasting Company, Inc.)

worthy *Wizards* during the latter 1960's. In New York City the Bil Baird Theatre presented a marionette *Wizard* from November 27, 1968, through March 2, 1969, and garnered high praise from reviewers. In 1974 the Smithsonian Puppet Theatre presented a marionette version of *The Marvelous Land of Oz* primarily on college campuses. Martin Williams' excellent script for the Smithsonian performances is completely faithful to the second Oz book. But for many Oz enthusiasts, the best puppet adaptations of Oz are those by Chicago artist Bill Eubank, whose versions have been performed in the Midwest since 1964. His elaborate marionettes are based upon Neill's illustrations, and his adaptations of the first two Oz books capture the spirit of the original.

Other than the Shirley Temple *Land*, there have been only three original Oz

Banner Elk, North Carolina, the Land of Oz amusement park. (Photograph Betty Dumbell)

Tip becomes Ozma. (Courtesy The National Broadcasting Company, Inc.)

Weeki Wachee Springs, Florida (1967); and even in the Ringling Bros. and Barnum & Bailey Circus (1965). The movie *Zardoz* takes its name and other ideas from *The Wizard of Oz,* though whether that is a tribute is hard to decide. And in 1970, the Land of Oz Park opened in Banner Elk, North Carolina; it features a dramatization in which children walk through at least some of Dorothy's adventures. Oz has appeared on television shows and television commercials. And there have been innumerable local performances of Oz dramas, some very elaborate.

Oz seems to appeal especially to puppeteers. The Reed Marionettes toured with an excellent show from 1963 through 1965, and the Royal European Marionette Theatre and Nicolo Marionettes each had note-

The Yellow Brick Road in the Banner Elk Oz park. (Photograph Betty Dumbell)

adaptations for television; two were produced by Videocraft International, and both were disasters. The earlier was *Tales of the Wizard of Oz*, a series of 130 four-and-a-half- to five-minute cartoons produced in 1960 and 1961 and syndicated for Saturday-morning broadcasts. There is continuity between each episode, though it is easy to lose track of what is happening. The cartoons bear almost no resemblance to Baum's story or to any other adaptation. Instead, they include trips to outer space, a heart for the Tin Man grown by planting "ruby-red rutabaga seeds," and the "brainless Munchkins," who swarm at inopportune moments and look somewhat akin to walking mushrooms, perhaps intentionally. On February 9, 1964, as its answer to the M-G-M movie, which CBS had shown the previous week, NBC presented the other Videocraft cartoon: an hour show entitled *Return to Oz*. The plot is distressingly

familiar; it seems that the Wicked Witch stole the Tin Woodman's heart, the Scarecrow's brains and the Cowardly Lion's courage, so with Dorothy they again journey to the Emerald City to ask the Wizard for help. Other plot complications ensue, interspersed with original songs. Both Videocraft projects use the same cartoon depictions, which show Dorothy and her comrades as especially dislikeable. *Return to Oz* was repeated by NBC on February 21, 1965; it has not been seen since.

Beginning on September 8, 1967, ABC presented its own Oz television show: *Off to See the Wizard,* with animations by M-G-M. The animations were quite good in a modernistic style, but the Oz portion of the program was relatively minor. Each broadcast showed the Oz characters going off to the Emerald City to see the Wizard; when they arrived there, he showed them a feature movie suitable for family viewing. The program lasted through the following spring.

Concluding this dismal decade for Oz dramatizations was the first feature for movie theaters since the M-G-M *Wizard*. This was *The Wonderful Land of Oz*, an adaptation of the second Oz book produced and directed by Barry Mahon for the Cinetron Corporation and released for matinées in the fall of 1969. The movie was especially poor, with clumsy directing and poor acting. It had, however, surprisingly good costumes.

Fortunately, the two most recent dramatizations go a long way to make up for the poor showing of the 1960's. The earlier of

Return to Oz, an animated cartoon, appeared on television in 1964. (Courtesy National Broadcasting Company, Inc.)

the two is Filmation's feature cartoon *Journey Back to Oz* (not to be confused with Videocraft's *Return to Oz*). Although production began in 1962, numerous financial difficulties delayed release until 1972 in England and Australia and 1974 in the United States, where it has appeared primarily in Saturday matinées. The cartoon is particularly interesting for featuring famous voices for each of the characters: Liza Minnelli (Dorothy), Margaret Hamilton (Aunt Em), Paul Ford (Uncle Henry), Ethel Merman (Mombi), Mickey Rooney (Scarecrow), Danny Thomas (Tin Man), Milton Berle (Cowardly Lion), Paul Lynde (Pumpkinhead), Risë Stevens (Glinda), Herschel Bernardi (Woodenhead the Horse) and Jack E. Leonard (Signpost). The dialogue is dull, and the songs are unmemorable. The animation, however, is excellent, and the adaptation of the second Oz book (with Dorothy taking the place of Tip and many other changes) is interesting. Mombi appears with green elephants to take over the Emerald City, and the elephants are very frightening, much more so than one expects from animations. *Journey Back to Oz* appeared on ABC television on December 5, 1976.

The other recent Oz dramatization is by far the most important since 1939. This is *The Wiz*, an all-black musical which opened on Broadway on January 5, 1975, after a road tour beginning the previous October. The Wiz bears no resemblance to the M-G-M movie or to any other dramatic version of *The Wonderful Wizard of Oz*, although the plot is surprisingly close to

the original. *The Wiz* is a combination of fine visual effects, modernistic choreography (including a Yellow Brick Road played by male dancers), black music ranging from lovely ballads (Aunt Em's "The Feeling We Once Had") to jazz parodies (the Wicked Witch's "Don't Nobody Bring Me No Bad News"). Twentieth Century-Fox, which financed the musical, should begin filming the movie version shortly.

We are too close to *The Wiz* to attempt a final judgment of it. In 1975 it deservedly won seven "Tony" awards, including that for Best Musical. Yet we wonder whether the parodistic element is too strong to make it entirely successful. For all the slickness and sentimentality of the 1939 movie, audiences never have much trouble in believing in the Oz it presents, even though it is never quite the Oz that Baum created. But it is almost impossible to believe that Dorothy in *The Wiz* ever went to a fantasy world with a good witch named Addaperle or a Tin Woodman with Miller High Life and Budweiser signs on his legs or a Wizard who dresses and acts like a rock hero (and does

it very well). *Gulliver's Travels*, like *The Wiz*, is a satire, but Jonathan Swift knew better than to let us question the existence of Lilliput and the Lilliputians and all the other strange places and peoples that Lemuel Gulliver visits.

After seventy-five years of Oz dramatizations, the early years dominated by the 1902 *Wizard of Oz* stage play, the later by Metro-Goldwyn-Mayer's 1939 *Wizard of Oz* movie, it will be interesting to see whether future adaptations will be influenced by *The Wiz*. It may not be too much to hope, however, that sometime there will be a major dramatic version of Oz that is entirely faithful to the world L. Frank Baum created. This has already been accomplished by puppeteers. Perhaps it can be captured on film or on the legitimate stage.

Otto Sarony Co.

1177 BROADWAY
NEW YORK

Ozian Artifacts

Chapter
5

Over the past seventy-odd years a surprising number of toys, games, dolls and other novelties depicting Oz characters have been manufactured. Aside from the "character merchandise" spawned by Walt Disney's films such as *Snow White* and *Pinocchio*, no other children's book has inspired so many manufactured novelties as *The Wizard of Oz*.

Dorothy, the Scarecrow, the Tin Woodman and the Cowardly Lion have been pictured on wall plaques and playing cards, book ends and bed sheets, silk scarfs and peanut-butter glasses. Their likenesses have appeared as stuffed dolls and plaster statuettes; they have been stamped in silver and sculpted in soap. All over the world their representations are almost as well known today as that of the ubiquitous Mickey Mouse.

The earliest known Oz novelties made their appearance on the evening of April 15, 1903. They were little brass jewel boxes with tiny Cowardly Lions mounted on their lids, presented to the ladies in the audience at the 100th performance of the musical comedy *The Wizard of Oz*. Metal folding-cup souvenirs marked the 200th performance of the play on July 11, and on several occasions little cardboard figures of the Scarecrow and the Tin Woodman were distributed to the children in the audience. There are known to have been postcard views of scenes from the play, and a few cards depicting some of the characters, which may have been part of a "rummy" game, but these were really advertisements.

The first Oz game was inspired by the Woggle-Bug contest of 1904 and was issued at that time or shortly thereafter by Parker Brothers, the Salem, Massachusetts, game manufacturers. *The Wogglebug Game of Conundrums* consisted of about a hundred question-and-answer cards based on standard riddles of the day. (Sample: "What

was Adam's favorite popular song?" "There's only one girl in the world for me.")

Considering the phenomenal popularity of the Oz books in the years that followed and the additional publicity provided by several silent movies and two more musical comedies based on Oz stories, it seems strange that no further Oz-inspired games or novelties appeared for some time, except for such publicity devices as Reilly & Britton's 1913 cardboard Rocking Woozy and a wooden Woozy manufactured in connec-

Early Oz novelties: *The Wogglebug Game* (circa 1905); *Little Oz Jig-Saw Puzzles* (1932); and *Wizard of Oz Waddle Book* (1934), with assembled Cowardly Lion, all ready to waddle.

THE WONDERFUL GAME of OZ

PARKER BROTHERS INC.
SALEM, MASS., NEW YORK, LONDON
Registered U.S. Patent Office

Two decorated glasses and a metal pail used by Swift's Oz peanut butter in the early 1960s. (Courtesy Justin G. Schiller)

tion with the Oz film company's 1914 *Patch work Girl of Oz* movie.

Then, in 1915, the Reilly & Britton Company issued *The Oz Toy Book*, designed by John R. Neill, which contained large full-color cutout figures of nearly fifty Oz characters printed on cardboard. The instruction page suggested that the figures might be mounted on stand-up bases and used to "act out the Oz stories." The book is a real rarity—only four complete copies are known to exist today.

In 1921 Parker Brothers issued *The Wonderful Game of Oz,* a parcheesi-like game whose folding playing-board was a large map of Oz, beautifully lithographed in colors, with all the Oz characters shown in their proper locations. There was a dice cup and cubes lettered W, I, Z, A, R and D, and the players—Dorothy, the Scarecrow, etc.—moved along the Yellow Brick Road according to their throws. The playing pieces were little pewter figurines. The game was reissued several times, most recently in 1939, when colored wood turnings replaced the more costly figurines.

In 1924 Frank Joslyn Baum began to manufacture a series of Oz dolls in Los Angeles. Made of printed Fabrikoid stuffed with kapok, they included the Scarecrow, the Tin Woodman, the Patchwork Girl and Jack Pumpkinhead, all carefully patterned after Neill's illustrations. The dolls were colorful and very attractive; but their manufacturer did not have the marketing experience or the means to compete with the arge toy concerns, and the venture failed. Young Baum arranged with the Oz book publishers (by then Reilly & Lee) to distribute his remaining stock, and for a single season in 1925 the company offered the dolls, each boxed with a copy of its own appropriate Oz book.

In 1932 Reilly & Lee decided to take advantage of the current jigsaw-puzzle craze and issued their *Little Oz Books with Jig Saw Oz Puzzles*. There were two different sets, each box containing two booklets and two die-cut jigsaw puzzles. The books were reissues of four of the 1913 *Little Wizard Series*, and the puzzles were made from the double-page illustration in each booklet.

A most ingenious novelty appeared in 1934. Blue Ribbon Books brought out, by arrangement with Bobbs-Merrill, *The Wizard of Oz Waddle Book*. This edition of *The Wizard* contained six die-cut cardboard inserts. When they were detached, Dorothy, Toto, the Scarecrow, the Tin Man, the Lion and the Wizard could be assembled as three-dimensional figures with metal springs attached to their legs so that they could be made to waddle down an inclined runway, which was furnished with the book. Copies of the *Waddle Book* with Waddles intact are extremely scarce today.

The second era of Oz artifacts began in 1939, when the M-G-M film inspired a bewildering mélange of Oz items. The prestigious Alexander Company of New York brought out engaging Scarecrows, Dorothys and stuffed-plush Cowardly Lions in several sizes. Smaller Oz character dolls, cast in rubber, squeaked when they were squeezed. There were also Oz charm bracelets, pencil boxes, coin purses, picture puzzles, writing paper, coloring books and greeting cards. A new *Wizard of Oz Game* was licensed by Loew's Inc. It was somewhat similar to the 1921 Parker Brothers one, although much cheaper and much less elaborate. Most of

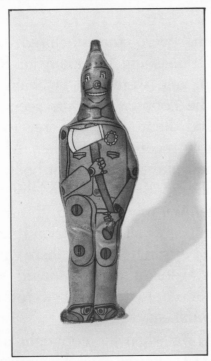

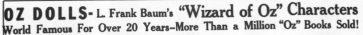

these items were manufactured by the Whitman Publishing Company of Racine, Wisconsin, and were sold in chain stores all over the country. Oz was seen everywhere—and heard everywhere, too, via phonograph records. But when M-G-M's *Wizard* had played out its last bookings in the neighborhood theaters and interest in the film temporarily subsided, the machinery turning out all this Ozian gadgetry came to a halt. In the 1940's there was only the Julian Wehr animated *Wizard*, a "toy book" with characters that were moved by tabs.*(Saalfield, 1944).*

In 1956, when the copyright on *The Wizard of Oz* expired, and the story and its characters went into public domain, the fun began. Various publishers issued new editions of the story, and there was an accompanying trickle of Oz toys and games. During the next decade the trickle became if not a flood, at least a steady stream that today shows no sign of abating.

The first optical Oz novelty appeared in 1957 when the Sawyer Company's View-Master Stereo Slides were issued. Their *Wizard of Oz* set consisted of three slides telling the story in twenty-one three-dimensional color photographs of sculptured character models placed in beautifully made settings. The Kenner Company produced a "Give-a-Show" projector, with color slides of storybook favorites, including the witch-melting episode from *The Wizard of Oz*. The Artistic Toy Company created a series of Oz dolls based on Videocrafts' 1962 TV cartoon series, *Tales of the Wizard of Oz*. In the same year Remco Industries brought out an intricate two-foot plastic showboat, complete with script book and miniature backdrops, scenery and cardboard characters for *The Wizard of Oz* and several other stories. Marx offered three *Off to See the Wizard* dancing dolls licensed by the 1967

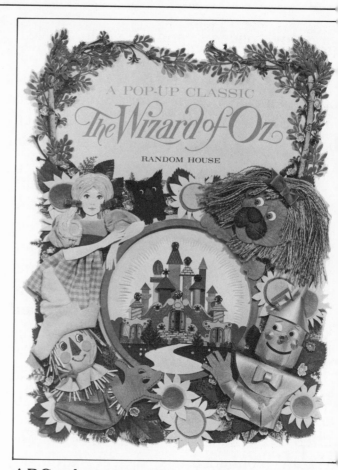

ABC television program; when wound up and placed on the floor, they spun in circles.

Random House published the first "Pop-up" *Wizard of Oz* in 1968. Halfway between a book and a toy, this colorful abridgment was a charming hodgepodge of pop-up scenes, manually operated animated figures and trick optical illusions. Mattel created an eerie little *Off to See the Wizard* glove puppet. It had a fabric body from which sprouted four plastic heads representing Dorothy and her three companions. When a string was pulled, one or another of the characters would talk (Tin Woodman: "Glunk, glunk—oil tastes good!"). In connection with its television sponsorship of the M-G-M movie in 1969, Procter & Gamble issued as premiums a set of well-modeled plastic puppets of the Oz characters, together with an attractive cardboard theater in the form of a castle. The New York Public Library sponsored manufacture of pewter figurines of the Oz characters, faithfully copied from Denslow's pictures. Aurora Plastics brought out a similar group of figurines with a few additional ones based on Neill's drawings and called them "Oz-kins." E. E. Fairchild, the Lowe Company and Milton Bradley all issued more or less elaborate *Wizard of Oz* board games. In recent years M-G-M has licensed numerous toys, games and even wastebaskets.

By 1970 one could build a collection of Oz jigsaw puzzles alone, or of Oz record albums. Oz wall decals, Oz music boxes, Oz bedspreads and Oz bath mats added to the colorful clutter in households of Oz enthusiasts across the country. Oz had become a land for all seasons, with Oz valentines, Oz Hallowe'en costumes and Oz Christmas-tree ornaments. Today, as testimony of the immortality of Oz, Glass Masters of New York offers stained-glass window panels of Dorothy, the Scarecrow, the Tin Woodman and the Cowardly Lion.

Nostalgia buffs and trivia collectors have long been attracted by the amazing variety of Ozian artifacts. The older items are avidly sought, and rare ones such as the 1921 Parker Brothers game bring high prices. But even the most recently manufactured Oz gadgets are quickly bought up and proudly displayed on collectors' shelves. The connoisseurs of rare editions of the Oz books, who generally disdain dolls and toys, are eager to acquire promotional items and souvenirs related to the publication of the books themselves.

Many Oz items are particularly desirable when they fall into "cross-collected" areas. For example, the elaborate Dorothy doll manufactured by Alexander in 1939 is attractive to doll collectors, Oz collectors and Judy Garland fans alike. But perhaps the most famous Oz artifacts ever to be collected were acquired in 1970, at M-G-M's auction of studio properties, for $15,000. They were the ruby slippers worn by Judy Garland in *The Wizard of Oz*.

Procter & Gamble Oz theater and puppets (1969).

Publisher's promotional material for *The Patchwork Girl of Oz* (1913) and *Kabumpo in Oz* (1922).

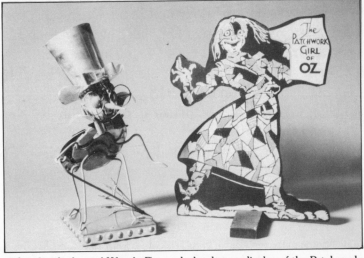

A handcrafted metal Woggle-Bug and a bookstore display of the Patchwork Girl. (Courtesy Justin G. Schiller)

THE OZ CANON*

(Listed below are the forty Oz books in the regular series, with their original publishers and illustrators.)

BY L. FRANK BAUM:

1. *The Wonderful Wizard of Oz*. Illustrated by W. W. Denslow. Chicago and New York: Geo. M. Hill Co., 1900. Reissued in 1903 by the Bobbs-Merrill Co. of Indianapolis as *The New Wizard of Oz*.

2. *The Marvelous Land of Oz*. Illustrated by John R. Neill. Chicago: The Reilly & Britton Co., 1904. Around 1906, the cover title was shortened to *The Land of Oz*, although it was not adopted on the title page until about 1914.

3. *Ozma of Oz*. Illustrated by John R. Neill. Chicago: The Reilly & Britton Co., 1907.

4. *Dorothy and the Wizard in Oz*. Illustrated by John R. Neill. Chicago: The Reilly & Britton Co., 1908.

5. *The Road to Oz*. Illustrated by John R. Neill. Chicago: The Reilly & Britton Co., 1909.

6. *The Emerald City of Oz*. Illustrated by John R. Neill. Chicago: The Reilly & Britton Co., 1910.

7. *The Patchwork Girl of Oz*. Illustrated by John R. Neill. Chicago: The Reilly & Britton Co., 1913.

8. *Tik-Tok of Oz*. Illustrated by John R. Neill. Chicago: The Reilly & Britton Co., 1914. Most of the plot of this book is from Baum's 1913 musical, *The Tik-Tok Man of Oz*, which in turn is a loose adaptation of the 1907 book, *Ozma of Oz*.

9. *The Scarecrow of Oz*. Illustrated by John R. Neill. Chicago: The Reilly & Britton Co., 1915. The plot of this book is in part from Baum's 1914 silent movie, *His Majesty, The Scarecrow of Oz*.

10. *Rinkitink in Oz*. Illustrated by John R. Neill. Chicago: The Reilly & Britton Co., 1916. This book was written around 1905 as *King Rinkitink* and was not originally an Oz book.

11. *The Lost Princess of Oz*. Illustrated by John R. Neill. Chicago: The Reilly & Britton Co., 1917.

12. *The Tin Woodman of Oz*. Illustrated by John R. Neill. Chicago: The Reilly & Britton Co., 1918.

13. *The Magic of Oz*. Illustrated by John R. Neill. Chicago: The Reilly & Lee Co., 1919.

14. *Glinda of Oz*. Illustrated by John R. Neill. Chicago: The Reilly & Lee Co., 1920.

*Some of the material in these lists comes from *Bibliographia Oziana, A Concise Bibliographical Checklist of the Oz Books by L. Frank Baum and His Successors* (published by the International Wizard of Oz Club in 1976), through the courtesy of the authors, Peter E. Hanff and Douglas G. Greene.

By Ruth Plumly Thompson:

15. *The Royal Book of Oz.* Illustrated by John R. Neill. Chicago: The Reilly & Lee Co., 1921. Although this book was published under Baum's name, it is entirely the work of Miss Thompson.

16. *Kabumpo in Oz.* Illustrated by John R. Neill. Chicago: The Reilly & Lee Co., 1922.

17. *The Cowardly Lion of Oz.* Illustrated by John R. Neill. Chicago: The Reilly & Lee Co., 1923.

18. *Grampa in Oz.* Illustrated by John R. Neill. Chicago: The Reilly & Lee Co., 1924.

19. *The Lost King of Oz.* Illustrated by John R. Neill. Chicago: The Reilly & Lee Co., 1925.

20. *The Hungry Tiger of Oz.* Illustrated by John R. Neill. Chicago: The Reilly & Lee Co., 1926.

21. *The Gnome King of Oz.* Illustrated by John R. Neill. Chicago: The Reilly & Lee Co., 1927.

22. *The Giant Horse of Oz.* Illustrated by John R. Neill. Chicago and New York: The Reilly & Lee Co., 1928.

23. *Jack Pumpkinhead of Oz.* Illustrated by John R. Neill. Chicago and New York: The Reilly & Lee Co., 1929.

24. *The Yellow Knight of Oz.* Illustrated by John R. Neill. Chicago and New York: The Reilly & Lee Co., 1930.

25. *Pirates in Oz.* Illustrated by John R. Neill. Chicago: The Reilly & Lee Co., 1931.

26. *The Purple Prince of Oz.* Illustrated by John R. Neill. Chicago: The Reilly & Lee Co., 1932.

27. *Ojo in Oz.* Illustrated by John R. Neill. Chicago: The Reilly & Lee Co., 1933.

28. *Speedy in Oz.* Illustrated by John R. Neill. Chicago: The Reilly & Lee Co., 1934.

29. *The Wishing Horse of Oz.* Illustrated by John R. Neill. Chicago: The Reilly & Lee Co., 1935.

30. *Captain Salt in Oz.* Illustrated by John R. Neill. Chicago: The Reilly & Lee Co., 1936.

31. *Handy Mandy in Oz.* Illustrated by John R. Neill. Chicago: The Reilly & Lee Co., 1937.

32. *The Silver Princess in Oz.* Illustrated by John R. Neill. Chicago: The Reilly & Lee Co., 1938.

33. *Ozoplaning with the Wizard of Oz.* Illustrated by John R. Neill. Chicago: Reilly & Lee, 1939.

By John R. Neill:

34. *The Wonder City of Oz.* Illustrated by John R. Neill. Chicago: Reilly & Lee, 1940.

35. *The Scalawagons of Oz.* Illustrated by John R. Neill. Chicago: Reilly & Lee, 1941.

36. *Lucky Bucky in Oz.* Illustrated by John R. Neill. Chicago: Reilly & Lee, 1942.

BY JACK SNOW:
37. *The Magical Mimics in Oz.* Illustrated by Frank Kramer. Chicago: The Reilly & Lee Co., 1946.
38. *The Shaggy Man of Oz.* Illustrated by Frank Kramer. Chicago: The Reilly & Lee Co., 1949.

BY RACHEL R. COSGROVE:
39. *The Hidden Valley of Oz.* Illustrated by "Dirk" [Dirk Gringhuis]. Chicago: The Reilly & Lee Co., 1951.

BY ELOISE JARVIS MCGRAW AND LAUREN MCGRAW WAGNER:
40. *Merry Go Round in Oz.* Illustrated by Dick Martin. Chicago: Reilly & Lee, 1963.

(Listed below are books which are generally considered Oz books but which are not part of the regular series.)

BY L. FRANK BAUM:

The Woggle-Bug Book. Illustrated by Ike Morgan. Chicago. The Reilly & Britton Co., 1905.

The Little Wizard Series. Six small volumes, each with 29 pages: *The Cowardly Lion and the Hungry Tiger, Little Dorothy and Toto, Tiktok and the Nome King, Ozma and the Little Wizard, Jack Pumpkinhead and the Sawhorse* and *The Scarecrow and the Tin Woodman.* Illustrated by John R. Neill. Chicago: The Reilly & Britton Co., 1913. Reissued in 1914 by Reilly & Britton as a single volume entitled *Little Wizard Stories of Oz.*

The Visitors from Oz. Illustrated by Dick Martin. Chicago: The Reilly & Lee Co., 1960. Heavily rewritten from Baum's 1904–5 comic page, *Queer Visitors from the Marvelous Land of Oz.*

BY W. W. DENSLOW:

Pictures from The Wonderful Wizard of Oz. Illustrated by W. W. Denslow. Chicago: George W. Ogilvie & Co., ca. 1903–4. This booklet consists of the original plates for the first edition of *The Wonderful Wizard of Oz,* with a new story by Thomas H. Russell.

Denslow's Scarecrow and The Tin-Man. Written and illustrated by W. W. Denslow. This story was issued both as a separate booklet and as part of a collected volume entitled *Denslow's Scarecrow and The Tin-Man and Other Stories.* New York: G. W. Dillingham Co., 1904.

BY JOHN R. NEILL:

The Oz Toy Book, Cut-Outs for the Kiddies. Chicago: The Reilly & Britton Co., 1915.

By "Frank Baum" [Frank Joslyn Baum]:

The Laughing Dragon of Oz. A Big Little Book. Illustrated by Milt Youngren. Racine, Wis.: Whitman Publishing Co., copyright 1934 but published January 11, 1935.

By Ruth Plumly Thompson:

Yankee in Oz. Illustrated by Dick Martin. [Kinderhook, Ill.]: The International Wizard of Oz Club, 1972.

The Enchanted Island of Oz. Illustrated by Dick Martin. [Kinderhook, Ill.]: The International Wizard of Oz Club, 1976.

By Jack Snow:

Who's Who in Oz. Illustrated by John R. Neill, Frank Kramer, and "Dirk" [Dirk Gringhuis]. Chicago: The Reilly & Lee Co., 1954.

Major Sources

(Serious students of Baum and Oz should consult the bibliography in *The Annotated Wizard of Oz* and the continuing listings in *The Baum Bugle.*)

The American Book Collector, December 1962. (Special L. Frank Baum issue.)
———, December 1964. (Special W. W. Denslow issue.)

Baum, Joan, and Roland Baughman. *L. Frank Baum. The Wonderful Wizard of Oz. An Exhibition of His Published Writings....* New York: Columbia University Libraries, 1956. (Primarily the work of Baughman.)

Baum, Frank Joslyn, and Russell P. MacFall. *To Please a Child, a Biography of L. Frank Baum....* Chicago: Reilly & Lee Co., 1961. (Primarily the work of MacFall.)

The Baum Bugle, 1957-current. Published three times each year by The International Wizard of Oz Club, P.O. Box 95, Kinderhook, Illinois 62345.

Ford, Alla T., and Dick Martin. *The Musical Fantasies of L. Frank Baum.* Chicago: The Wizard Press, 1958.

Gardner, Martin, and Russel B. Nye. *The Wizard of Oz and Who He Was.* East Lansing: Michigan State University Press, 1957.

Greene, Douglas G., and Michael Patrick Hearn. *W. W. Denslow.* Mt. Pleasant, Michigan: Clarke Historical Library, Central Michigan University, 1976.

Hanff, Peter E., and Douglas G. Greene. *Bibliographia Oziana: A Concise Bibliographical Checklist of the Oz Books by L. Frank Baum and His Successors.* Kinderhook, Illinois: The International Wizard of Oz Club, 1976.

Hearn, Michael Patrick. *The Annotated Wizard of Oz....* New York: Clarkson N. Potter, 1973.

McClelland, Doug. *Down the Yellow Brick Road: The Making of The Wizard of Oz.* New York: Pyramid Books, 1976. (About the 1939 Metro-Goldwyn-Mayer *Wizard of Oz* movie.)

Moore, Raylyn. *Wonderful Wizard, Marvelous Land.* Bowling Green, Ohio: Bowling Green University Popular Press, 1974.

Snow, Jack. *Who's Who in Oz.* Chicago: The Reilly & Lee Co., 1954.

Wagenknecht, Edward. *Utopia Americana.* University of Washington Chapbooks No. 28. Seattle: University of Washington Bookstore, 1929.

About the Authors

DAVID L. GREENE earned his doctorate in English literature at the University of Pennsylvania and is currently chairman of the English Department at Piedmont College, Demorest, Georgia. He has been active in the International Wizard of Oz Club since its inception in 1957. He has been on the editorial staff of its journal since 1968 and was editor in chief from 1968 to 1973. He is co-author of the introduction to a new edition of Baum's 1901 fantasy, *The Master Key,* and has edited an anthology of Baum's shorter fairy tales, *The Purple Dragon and Other Fantasies.* His article "The Concept of Oz" appeared in Vol. 3 of *Children's Literature,* and he is working on a collection of critical articles about Baum and Oz.

A native Chicagoan, DICK MARTIN is a professional artist with experience ranging from newspaper cartooning to carnival-banner painting. He attended the School of the Art Institute of Chicago and the Chicago Academy of Fine Arts. His career has been linked to the Land of Oz since his childhood days, when he was so impressed by the fanciful Oz book illustrations that he determined to be an illustrator himself. To date he has illustrated more than a dozen juveniles, one of which, *The Littlest Star,* won him a Top Honor award in the Chicago Book Clinic's 1961 exhibit of Chicago and Midwestern bookmaking. His credits also include several Oz books, among them *The Visitors from Oz* and *Merry Go Round in Oz.* While doing the research for an Oz monograph he became involved with the International Wizard of Oz Club, and was editor of its magazine for several years.

Acknowledgments

We are greatly indebted to Harvey Plotnick, president of the Henry Regnery Company (successor to Reilly & Britton and Reilly & Lee), for many courtesies and for permission to reproduce Oz illustrations and publicity. We are also grateful to the Baum family for kindnesses stretching over many years, especially to L. Frank Baum's grandsons, Dr. Robert A. Baum, Sr., and Joslyn S. Baum; his great-grandson, Robert A. Baum, Jr.; and his niece, Miss Matilda J. Gage. We are indebted to the late Ruth Plumly Thompson not only for her twenty-one Oz books but also for friendship over the past two decades, innumerable wise and witty letters, and her ability to tolerate her many adult enthusiasts with unfailing good humor.

We are also indebted to Martin Gardner for his suggestion that this book be written; to Dr. Douglas G. Greene and Peter E. Hanff for supplying reproductions and for permission to use material in *Bibliographia Oziana;* to Justin G. Schiller for reproductions from his superb collection; to Irene Fisher for lending material for reproduction; to John Van Camp for his enthusiasm and invaluable assistance in making photographs; to Rachel Cosgrove Payes, Eloise Jarvis McGraw and Lauren McGraw Wagner for information about their contributions to the Oz series; to Ray Powell and Robin Olderman for information about Oz toys and games; to Dr. Jerry V. Tobias, editor in chief of *The Baum Bugle,* for permission to use material from that journal; to Betty Dumbell for photographs of the Land of Oz Park, Banner Elk, South Carolina; and to Elizabeth L. Greene for her patience and encouragement. Others whose assistance we gratefully acknowledge include: Martin Williams; Michael Barrier; Michael Patrick Hearn; Norman Ginsburg, Director, Information Services, CBS Radio; National Broadcasting Company Archives; American Broadcasting Company Archives; American Literature Collection, Beinecke Rare Book and Manuscript Library, Yale University Library; Rare Book Division, the New York Public Library, Astor, Lennox and Tilden Foundations; Theatre Collection, the New York Public Library at Lincoln Center, Astor, Lennox and Tilden Foundations; Chicago Historical Society; Western Publishing Company; Parker Brothers; Metro-Goldwyn-Mayer, Inc.; and the staff of the Northeast Georgia Regional Library, Clarkesville, Georgia.

Special thanks are due to those who have worked with us at Random House: Robert Aulicino, designer of this book; Sarah Leslie and Betsy Amster; Linda Marshall, whose research for us at NBC was invaluable; and most especially our editor, Anne Freedgood, who suffered with us through the writing of this book, who shepherded it through the press, and who tolerated more from her authors than any editor should have to put up with — all with infinite courtesy and sympathy.

D.L.G.
D.M.